SCIENCE
AND
RELIGION

What you were never told

Dr. Kasem Khaleel

KNOWLEDGE HOUSE
Buffalo Grove, Illinois

Table of Contents

Introduction

Today, science and religion are regarded as completely separate concepts. It is commonly believed that the sciences and faith in God are polarized, perhaps antagonistic. No scientist would ever consider combining them. The idea of a God is purposely separated from the sciences. In fact, the majority of scientists frown on the concept that everything is attributable to a divine being. It is unpopular to even mention the name of God in concert with scientific advancement. However, there was a time when God's name was mentioned in the advancement of the sciences. Yet, the current thinking is that belief in God and belief in the sciences are impossible to reconcile.

Often, scientists refuse to even consider the possibility of a creator of the universe. In the classroom the idea of a creative and involved God is regarded as unacceptable. Certainly, there is enormous resistance to the mention of God, especially in regard to scientific discoveries. In the classroom today it is inconceivable that a person could mention a great discovery, like the finding of ice on Mars, and then give credit to a creator. This would evoke a reprimand from teachers.

The question is why are people in authority resistant to the idea of a creative God? What's more, why are they openly hostile to the mention of His name? These would appear to be emotional reactions rather than rational, that is scientific, ones. This is what the scientist Robert Jastrow proposes in his book, *God and the Astronomers*. He states that when presented with the claim for the existence of an all-powerful, universal creator astronomers routinely become emotionally agitated for no logical reason.

There are those who would claim that the mention of God is unscientific. Yet, no evidence is provided for such a view. In other words, the evidence which disproves the role or existence of an all-powerful Creator is severely lacking. Incredibly, as mentioned previously in scientific meetings, as well as in the classroom, the mention of God in any respect is frowned upon. Certainly, it is never encouraged.

Science is unable to explain how living beings originated. Nor can it explain what happens after death. These issues are strictly matters of faith. Yet, creation and death are crucial, because they help human beings understand their origins as well as their ultimate destinies. Simply claiming that no God exists because He is impossible to physically see or claiming that upon death nothing else will happen is unscientific, that is if science is truly based upon organized thinking. In fact, such an approach is more unscientific than claiming proof for the existence of a God. This is because the universe provides unlimited evidence for the existence of an all-powerful creator, as will be demonstrated throughout this book.

A more scientific approach is to analyze the possible existence of a Supreme Being through the use of reason. Then, the individual can methodically assess the possibilities: Does a creative power exist, or is the current view correct, which is there is no evidence for or need of such a vital force? Was there perhaps originally a God, but He is no longer involved? In other words, if eons ago there was a creator, is this Being now inactive? If such a belief is held, is this belief based upon reason? Or, is it based upon personal desires, for instance, the desire to avoid a sense of responsibility to a higher power? Or, could He truly be thoroughly and actively involved in the universe as well as in our very lives?

Is there evidence within this vast universe for the existence of an all-powerful being? Or, is there firm evidence indicating the lack of such an existence? Consider the degree of order found in this universe. Is there any other possibility besides the involvement of an almighty Creator? From the obvious it is under a mighty and universal control. In contrast, is there even a minute degree of evidence indicating that this universe lacks a controlling being? Are there any scientific experiments which indicate that it is self-sufficient? Can science support the idea that a creator is unnecessary?

This is far from an attempt to prove the existence of God scientifically. Rather, it is merely a challenge to test science's position. In other words, are statements being made because of certain peoples' personal views? Is the view of denying the role of God based upon a specific agenda? Millions, perhaps billions, of people willingly deny God's ever-present role. Yet, what a catastrophe it would be if one's understanding was based solely on the views of others, who are themselves biased. In other words, regarding the modern thinking of the existence of a creator are personal agendas the source of the attitudes? Or, has a logical, that is scientific, analysis been made?

Modern science has dealt with the issue of a God from the vantage point of vested interests. It has consistently maintained a special agenda, that is to minimize, even neutralize, the idea of a creator. In scientific meetings if God's name is mentioned, hostility, anger, or at a minimum apathy and skepticism are expected. Scientists have been particularly hostile to the concept of a highly active God, that is a being who is systematically involved in all aspects of human and celestial existence. Incredibly, scientists' personal views and even their desires for financial gain motivate the anti-divine (no need for God) position.

The claim is that there is no need for a God, because all that is needed is good science. From this it would appear that science is self-sufficient. Scientists can do their experiments at will, and, seemingly, they are completely independent of need. How science alone could be self-sufficient is never explained.

Yet, scientists are definite on one point. It is that an involved God is unnecessary. Nor is God's existence regarded as provable. However, those who maintain these views have never analyzed scientifically, that is systematically, the possible existence of an active, viable God. In other words, the claims are made without substantiation. Thus, the current view among scientists, that there is no persistently active God, Who is involved in every aspect of human existence, is at best a theory. Yet, incredibly, scientists often represent this theory as if it were fact, making claims such as "The universe operates by chance," or "evolution develops on its own—no God is needed," or, possibly, "If there was a creator, He is no longer involved, since the world evolves on its own." Incredibly, scientists make these claims, even though they provide no evidence for their positions. The fact is these statements are highly emotional. Such claims violate the very basis of science, which is to avoid making statements until firm evidence is procured. Therefore, by science's own definition such statements are unfounded.

Yet, regarding those who completely deny His existence the question arises: Is there even the slightest degree of evidence supporting such a position? Even if physical proof for a God is lacking, that is the ability to physically see or sense Him, is this, from a scientific point of view, sufficient basis to deny him? These are issues which require serious consideration, particularly before excluding the possible existence of an almighty God. This is because if such a God exists, the blatant denial of Him would be catastrophic, that is in the individual's personal life. It is catastrophic even for the scientist. This is because science is supposedly based upon the use of reason, and a blanket denial of His existence prior to using reason violates its premise. Yet, more critically, it is catastrophic because of the degree of personal loss that will result. Think about it. If a loving yet all powerful and demanding God exists, a God Who expects human loyalty, and the person denies Him, could there be any greater catastrophe?

Yet, ultimately, the point is why deny Him when there is no need to do so? Who else is there to recognize, in other words, are there any other options? Are there any significant alternatives? Are there any other proven power sources? Regarding the ultimate destiny of humans—that phase after death—is there any other possibility besides returning to Him? Could human beings exist without a Helper and Assistant, without a Source, which provides for all? On this planet everything that is needed is provided. Regarding this denial of God: Who else could have created humans, and Who else could maintain the supports and systems upon which humans depend? The catastrophe of denying Him is made evident from a simple concept: Who made this incredibly vast world and universe which surrounds us, star upon star and galaxy upon galaxy, universe upon universe? This world and the infinite universe about us is highly organized. It is also systematic and predictable. The fact that it is predictable certainly indicates the existence of an almighty control. It is indisputable that the universe continuously operates in perfection. Therefore, Who made it, and Who keeps it functioning? Is it God, or is it pure, raw chance?

Chapter One

Law and Order:
The Way of the Universe

Everything in existence follows specific laws. These laws were surely created by a force that is highly intelligent. Laws simply cannot develop on their own.

All scientists know that living beings adhere to specific patterns or laws. They also know that these laws are predictable. Non-living substances also follow certain laws. The operations of the earth and moon, as well as the vast universe, are based upon them. What's more, as is agreed by all scientists these laws are highly systematic. In other words, they follow a specific pattern, which is highly organized.

The earth and the universe operate strictly by following the laws of science. George Smoot notes in his book, *Wrinkles in Time*, that the universe follows systems at all levels, atomic to galactic. The question is who made these laws? What's more, since they are so orderly, could they have developed merely by chance?

Nothing can become organized by itself. Someone— some unfathomable powerful Being—must make the effort. Thus, it appears that this universe, as well as this very earth, is under the control of a universal Master, Who singlehandedly operates it. This Master would be a Force of sorts, a Being of incomprehensible nature, one that, in fact, produces the laws which rule all that exists. Then, this is that ultimate Power, which not only originated whatever exists but also governs it. It is a Being Who is truly inventive, because He alone creates the laws upon which all sustenance, as well as scientific achievement, is based.

There must be such a Force. It is a Force which maintains law and order. While impossible to visualize, such an all-powerful being must exist, because, as is evident from life here, law and order are required for survival. The same must hold true for the universe, that is its survival is dependent upon pre-arranged laws. In other words, God made the laws, applied them, and, then, maintains them. The universe is too orderly to be devoid of such an active organizer. Without pre-arranged laws it could never be so utterly organized. In fact, without such an all-controlling power the universe would disintegrate into nothingness.

In this life everything follows specific laws. The planets and stars of this galaxy, the galaxy itself, adhere to unalterable rules. In other words, there is absolute law and order in this universe. For instance, regarding its celestial motion the earth follows precise and undeniable laws. This galaxy itself, the Milky Way, follows a totally predictable and highly organized pattern. Within it billions of celestial bodies operate in a highly systematic fashion. As well, the human body functions completely by laws, which are highly organized as well as predictable. Plants and animals are born, then live and die, all through these same laws. Thus, everything in existence, everything that we know of, is under the control of a powerful force. Nothing develops on its own or merely by chance. Moreover, scientists have thoroughly proven that the universe follows a specific, predictable system of law and order. They have also proven that it never operates by chance and that, in fact, the latter leads to disorganization, rather, utter destruction. What's more, experience demonstrates that nothing can be created by accident. In other words, it takes a specific effort to create a thing. For instance, in the laboratory whatever is produced or "created" requires a specific and highly controlled effort. What's more, in order for the effort to be successful there is always someone in charge. Wouldn't it be the same for the universe? As the epitome of hypocrisy scientists claim that the universe operates on its own, while these same individuals purport that scientific efforts must be highly organized, extensively monitored, and pre-planned.

Every scientist knows that before any system or experiment can be created, a design—a specific plan—is required. What's more, someone must create the design. Someone must organize the details. Thus, there must be a specific plan before it can proceed. In other words, systems never arise by accident. This is true in all aspects of this world. Businessmen know that leaving issues to chance leads to financial disaster. To be successful they must consistently design for the future. They must create specific, well-ordered plans to fully succeed. Chemists are aware that relying on chance results in experimental failure. Experiments must be conducted according to specific rules. What's more, exact measurements must be adhered to. Minute errors greatly influence the outcome. Unless precision is maintained, failure results.

Biologists know that all growth and development, whether plant or animal, depends upon organized controls. They realize that all living beings abide by specific systems. Plus, they know that they are managed by a controlling force. What's more, they are fully aware that biological growth is energy dependent. For instance, all plant growth is dependent upon the energy from the sun, that is solar rays. The plants absorb these rays, which spurs growth. The mechanism is that the sun produces highly energized particles, known as photons, which are pure energy. These particles are directly absorbed by the plants, and, thus, growth is stimulated. This is known as photosynthesis. This method of plant energy production is thoroughly organized and predictable. The fact is in biology, in terms of how things operate, accidents are unknown. Rather, living beings operate via a highly specific and organized design. It is a specific plan that is impossible to alter. Thus, nature operates through organization. The laws it follows are predictable. Biology can always be depended upon to respond in a systematic way.

There is nothing humans can do to alter its mechanisms. In biology untold thousands of life forms, each with its own unique design, are known. In this wide variety of organisms there is a universal scheme. Universally, these living beings adhere to a system of precise laws. There are no exceptions to this rule. Whatever happens on this earth, there is proof for the existence of a design. Think of a power plant. It makes energy through a specific and well planned effort. It is completely dependent upon humans, who organize the effort. In other words, if left to chance, no power would be generated. Someone must always be in control. Similarly, when factory workers create merchandise, they do so through an organized effort. The fact is their approach must be completely systematic. Any disruption in the organization, any deficiency in the effort, and any deviation in the system leads to inferior results and/or faulty merchandise. The same must hold true for the universe surrounding us. An inadequate effort, that is a poorly organized and executed plan, would result in "universal" mayhem. Yet, the universe is precisely the opposite of chaos or accidental events, since, as any amateur observer can see, it is free of faults. Thus, there must be an Organizational Power behind it. In other words, there must exist a Designer, who manages and controls all. Such a designer is far from a remote force. He is, in fact, actively involved in all aspects of His design, from the most minute detail to the most massive, critical event.

Energized and Organized—The Visible Universe

The question arises, what force generates the power for the magnificent universe surrounding us? The coal or oil that produces heat in a furnace represents raw energy. What's more, it took human energy to extract it from the earth. However, over the course of untold eons vast amounts of energy were required to produce these concentrated fuels. The ultimate source of energy to make them is extraterrestrial: solar radiation.

Plants require energy from the sun. They also require nourishment from rain, which activates growth. Rain water is crucial, because it puts minerals into solution, so they can be absorbed by the plants. Minerals are essential for plant growth.

Minerals make up a significant proportion of this universe. Represented by over one hundred different types, they exist ubiquitously in nature. How they were created is largely unknown. Human beings are incapable of making them. They originate from universal, that is extraterrestrial, sources, the current thinking being that they were fathered ultimately from solar hydrogen and helium.

Plants are also a source of mineral matter. When their energy source is exhausted, that is when they are no longer able to synthesize energy, they die. Eventually, their residues decay into the soil and, therefore, add to its mineral content. Ultimately, they become fuel for the future: gas, oil, and/or coal. Then, this is used as energy for innumerable purposes. It is the energy by which humans survive today. Through it, humans thrive. Without it, humans degenerate, perhaps die. Thus, on earth it is energy—power—that drives everything. If the power is taken away, human existence, as well as the existence of every other living being, would cease. Could it be any different for the universe at large?

Only a mighty universal Power can create. Only an unfathomable supernatural Source can generate energy, endlessly so, from nothing. Despite every possible attempt humans are incapable of creating energy from a void. Thus, could energy haphazardly develop on its own within the universe? What's more, where did the idea of energy originate? Untold trillions of tons of energy are produced in this universe every day, all of which serve productive purposes. Surely, the existence of such energy could only be the result of an omnipotent creator.

Regardless of the greatness of its advances science has yet to create. Nor can it produce raw energy from a void, as obviously occurs within the universe.

Science has proven that the universe is highly organized. It has demonstrated that it, along with the earth, operates through predictable systems. Yet, how did it become so? The universe is utterly systematic. Thus, does it make sense that it could have developed strictly by chance, without an Operational Force, which controls all? While the scope or magnitude of such a Force may be impossible to comprehend, does this preclude its existence, regardless of how mind-boggling such a creature seems?

True, chaos does happen in the universe. At any time absolute destruction may occur. A star may explode, obliterating planets and everything else in its path. The earth itself could be destroyed, for instance, by an errant asteroid or comet. Thus, chaos is created. Yet, the key word is *created*. However, even a destructive force of such a degree must adhere to specific, predictable laws.

Science itself begins as chaos, that is the chaos of an unproven theory. It begins as the chaos of human thought. It is within the thought process that the possible cause or truth behind a certain issue is suspected. However, experiments are required to provide the proof. To perform the appropriate experiment the scientist must organize his thoughts. A plan must be devised. Then, he or she must decide on a course of action and proceed in a specific direction. Thus, through an organized effort science must first prove the accuracy and truth of an issue before it can proceed.

This is conceivably how the Master of the Universe operates, in a sense like humans. Just as humans must make an effort to maintain systems, the Universal Being must also do so. Humans know that effort is needed to maintain organization. Constant work must be expended to keep systems functioning optimally. Any disruption or insufficiency leads to deficient results. Even the slightest degree of neglect results in disorganization and disrepair.

Think about it. Is there a single aspect of life, which, if neglected, can operate properly? The fact is neglect always leads to destruction. Regarding the monumental and infinite universe could there be any other option besides the fact that an organizer and worker is required? Consider this: how could humans, animals, plants, planets, stars, galaxies, or anything else exist on their own? Every aspect of life on this earth requires support, help, and organization. Could it be different for the endless universe? Therefore, the only logical conclusion is that there is a God and this God is thoroughly active and aware. What's more, the major difference is that while human beings eventually become exhausted from their efforts, God almighty never wears out.

To create or organize human efforts energy is required. Science is merely a system, never an energy source. The fact is all scientific experiments require energy. First, a scientist must conceive of the experiment, a process that requires mental energy. Such mental activity itself is regarded as an electrical or wave energy. Yet, energy is also needed for the devices and instruments used to perform experiments. Thus, scientific efforts are completely dependent upon energy sources. When energy or power is applied, be it the energy of electricity or that of the muscles of the human hand, results are produced. Without energy, everything stalls.

Regarding the organization of the universe, as well as its maintenance, there must also be a Power Source. The fact is such a power must be a vital living being, who is in absolute and constant control. Without it the universe, like all other systems, would fall into disrepair, rather, fulminant chaos. In fact, it would cease to exist.

There are those who might accept that, originally, there was a creative Power: God created the universe. However, as this thinking continues there is no longer any need for such a God, whether by the vast universe or humankind. The universe, and, specifically, our lives, are free of reliance upon Him. Everything operates on its own, that is by mere accident. Yet, this view too is largely irrational, based upon an individual's personal view, or personal wishes, rather than any scientific rationale.

How this operates can be understood through what happens in this very world. Imagine starting an experiment such as a simple chemistry procedure. What if, suddenly, the procedure was halted and no further chemicals were added? Wouldn't the experiment utterly fail? What about, for instance, the most grand experiment of all: the creation of the universe? What if, after initiating this magnificent "model," no further effort was exerted, that is if, suddenly, all effort was halted? What if in its maintenance no further energy was expended? What would remain except utter chaos or, at a minimum, a useless residue? Anyone who conducts experiments knows that if an experiment is halted midway, the result is disaster. What's more, for the experiment to be completed there must be a continuous effort to maintain control. Strict protocols must be followed. The slightest deviation results in experimental failure. If this is true in the earthly experience, what about the vast universe? In fact, without an all-controlling power that continuously and tirelessly administers, that cohesively maintains both structure and function, the universe would self-destruct. This is indisputable.

The fact that this is a universe which has been specifically designed would indicate that, in fact, there must be a Designer. Such a Designer would be utterly wise and magnificent, beyond any conceivable representation. This designer would be the creator of the vast universe: God almighty Himself.

Chapter Two

Atoms, Microbes, and More:
A Chance Event?

Through science humans have been able to reach fantastic heights. They have created phenomenal inventions. Yet, despite the enormity of these advancements there is one arena where science is impotent: the creation of life. For scientists the creation of a living entity has proven utterly elusive. The fact is by human hands not even a single biological system has been created, for instance, the living enzyme, a piece of DNA, or a human cell. Nor have scientists been able to create even something more simplistic such as the building block of all existence: the atom.

Certainly, atoms and molecules can be altered. What's more, molecules can be synthesized, for instance, certain hormones and vitamins. However, the atomic materials used to synthesize them—the inorganic or organic raw materials, for instance, a molecule of sodium or calcium, the living enzyme, and/or DNA—are impossible to produce. Nor is it possible to conceive of the method to design such substances. Anything more sophisticated, such as genes, chromosomes, cells, or

microbes, are so torturously complex that scientists are
unable to fathom even the slightest degree of their
manufacture. Regardless of the effort they are impossible to create. True, genes can be altered, or rather,
corrupted, as is occurring through the so-called genetic
engineering. However, these genes are impossible to
manufacture synthetically. What's more, certainly,
scientists are utterly incapable of making new life, that
is to invent an unknown creation. Yet, the Power
behind the universe, that being known as almighty
God, routinely creates the unknown.

As an illustration of the impotence of the human creative ability scientists are utterly incapable of producing
even the lowly microbe. Such an organism has never
been artificially produced, not even remotely so. Nor is
there any evidence that it could develop accidentally.
What are the odds that all of its components could spontaneously organize themselves together to form an intelligent organism? They are nil. Then, Who created it?
While minuscule, the microbe has a highly complicated
structure. Then, could it have developed accidentally, or
is there a Power behind it, creating, organizing, controlling and re-creating it? All that is necessary to disprove
accidental creation is to look at a microbe under a micro-
scope. Obviously, such a being couldn't develop by
accident. Rather, it is highly organized, operating with
utter precision. In other words, like all other life forms it
follows its own predictable and specific plan. It never
operates by chance. Nor does it deviate from the laws
which govern it. Furthermore, it is utterly impossible for

scientists to make genetic material let alone an entire living organism. Thus, despite all of today's scientific expertise, not even the tiniest living being can be created. Then, who made such beings?

All living beings are highly complex, beyond imagination. A single cell is so complicated that it is truly unfathomable. It is unfathomable regarding how it works so efficiently and perfectly to perform its unique functions. What's more, there exists an infinite variety of cells: each is unique. For instance, the live bark of a tree, that is the bark found under the outer and dry surface, is made of vital, living cells. Each tree has its own special type of bark. Each even has its own special type of cellular fluid, i.e. protoplasm. Amazingly, the outer bark is synthesized in this fluid protoplasm, which builds these hard walls for its cells (and then dies). Animal cells are even more complicated. The human brain contains cells, which store sensations, keeping a type of biological record. Other brain cells are essentially living switchboards, which send critical messages. In a mere square inch the human blood contains up to seventy billion cells, all of which perform highly specialized functions. None of this could occur by chance. All of it fits a well-ordered design.

Energy: A Divine Creation?

Everything in existence requires energy. No earthly experiment can proceed without it. Laboratory experiments require a variety of energy sources, human and mechanical. Wouldn't the same hold true for the vast universe or the very earth upon which we live? Someone must create the energy which sustains it. If the rules for the need of a power source hold true for whatever occurs on this planet, could it be any different for the universe at large? The fact is it takes energy to create, especially living beings—vast energy. The question is where does that energy come from? DNA, that is the unique genetic material: does it have the energy or ability to organize itself? If not, what is its energy source? What's more, who created its incredibly intricate and systematic design? The fact is it is far too complex and organized to develop merely by chance. All biologists and mathematicians know this. Thus, it makes sense that behind it there is a mighty Designer, one Who is so utterly intelligent and capable in His designing that He is unfathomable: almighty God, the Lord, Master, and Creator of the infinite universe.

Science and God: From the Same Source?

Modern scientists refuse to acknowledge the involvement in this universe of an overriding divine power. Incredibly, in Western schools there has been a concerted effort to eliminate from the curriculum the idea of a creative and involved God, especially in the sciences. This is despite the fact that science is supposedly based upon facts. In other words, it claims to be unbiased and unemotional. Yet, a factual basis for the elimination of a creative power is severely lacking. Rather, the operations of the universe, which are so utterly organized and thoroughly complete that they defy comprehension, clearly support the idea of an ultimate and divine power. This is why from a scientific, that is rational, point of view science and religion are compatible. If the concepts of belief are based upon whatever originates from the universe's creator, then it must be true. The fact is since the universe operates by a specific design, to deny and exclude the possibility of the Designer is itself unscientific.

Science is based upon the possibility of discovering the truth, because it uses experiments to prove or disprove theories. If the theories are proven correct, then they are accepted as potentially true. Yet, in many instances despite potential evidence they remain theories, because 100% certainty is unattainable. For instance, the physical structure of the atom remains unknown. No one knows for sure what it looks like or precisely how it functions. Thus, the atomic structure, which is the very basis for much of modern science, remains theoretical. Therefore, it is not an absolute truth. This is an excellent example of the greatest deficiency of modern science: its inability to determine absolute truth. This does not mean science is incapable of determining certain truths. If it accumulates enough proof, the truth can be established. However, even if theories are accepted as true, like the theories for the origin or extinction of the dinosaurs, usually there is never enough evidence to prove them absolutely.

In religion this potential for discovering the truth can also hold true. If its concepts truly originate from a superhuman source—almighty God Himself—then they should make sense, that is they should withstand investigative scrutiny. If they fail to arise from Him, then they should be easily disproved. In this case it could be presumed that they are human fabrications.

Even with religion, faith in a specific issue should be based upon more than just emotions. Reason should be the basis for arriving at an individual's beliefs as well as for understanding the role played by an ever-present, all-powerful creator. The fact is if reason were applied as the basis for belief in God, the commitment to His almighty self would be greatly enhanced. What's more, there would be a more profound understanding of the nature of God as would be the understanding of the afterlife. The adherence to His rules and laws would be more resolute. What's more, there would be a greater degree of cooperation among people of different religions or beliefs. This is because rather than being based upon emotions such interactions would be based upon rational thinking. In other words, rather than reacting with "feelings" the reaction would be based upon careful thought. As a result, people would interact in a superior way. What's more, the degree of tolerance between people would dramatically rise. Even in matters regarded purely as spiritual, such as certain rituals, if reason were applied, there would be greater tolerance and understanding, perhaps even greater compliance. In contrast, if an issue of faith was based upon fraud, the use of reason could help determine the error. Thus, the individual could arrive closer to the truth. This may explain why certain religions fear the introduction of reason. Yet, reason fails to diminish faith. Rather, it strengthens it. The fact is a thorough understanding of the workings of God results in an even more profound degree of commitment than belief based merely upon ritual. In contrast, ignorance perpetuates disbelief, in fact, creates it. It weakens commitment, causing religion to become a burden. Thus, religion is dreaded, in fact, loathed.

The Renaissance, in which Europe was rescued from its intellectual quagmire, was based upon reason. The fact is blind faith was largely the cause of Europe's stagnation. Events in the Dark Ages were largely emotionally driven. Because ignorance was so pervasive, the populace was readily manipulated. Ignorance results in repression. In fact, it perpetuates the utter decay of humanity. If there is a failure to rely upon reason, people stop evaluating issues. Behavioral patterns are never questioned. The causes for the rise and decline of civilization are never investigated. Thus, the status quo, whether correct or erroneous, is accepted. As a result, human advancement stalls. Therefore, today, people of faith who fail to use their reason, whether Muslim, Christian, or Jew, remain in decay. Paganism infiltrates what were once true practices. As a result, religions are created, which bear little or no resemblance to the original truth. What's more, questionable practices are adhered to, and no one even contests them.

Yet, if the intellect were relied upon to determine the relevancy, as well as accuracy, of certain practices, errant or deviant concepts would be discarded. Yet, when issues regarding religion arise, usually the reactions are emotional. Incredibly, according to the Qur'an the first aspect to consider is to use the intellect, that is to rely upon the innate intelligence, to pursue religion. What's more, it claims the only true religion is the sincere worship of almighty God. It also stresses the importance of reaching an understanding of the nature of God through the use of reason. However, regardless of the affiliation in religious circles today rarely is such a concept emphasized. In fact, today, there is often a lack of tolerance, even violence, against certain peoples, merely because of their beliefs. This would indicate that poverty of the mind, that is illiteracy and backwardness, results in utter depravity, regardless of religious affiliation. Thus, through the active use of the mind the understanding of God, as well as the human relationship to Him, is enhanced. From the spiritual point of view this makes sense. He created the human brain, and He alone established the capacity to think. He created the very plan, the neurological blueprint, for constructing the brain. Thus, He alone knows how it truly operates. This is why it is reasonable to presume that the deeper a person thinks, the closer he or she will come to God. Correspondingly, the less a person thinks—the less actively he or she uses the mind—the further from God he or she will become. Thus, by definition ignorance and/or illiteracy is equivalent with disbelief, while learning is synonymous with faith, worship, and true belief. This is because if the individual understands the reason and value of what he/she adheres to, that is the actual benefits he or she will attain, faith in a divine being, or even the adherence to ritual, will be solidified. In fact, the degree of faith will dramatically increase. What's more, it will likely be based upon an issue utterly profound: knowledge rather than emotional attachment. Whatever people pursue in life it is the benefits which draw them. Why would it be different with God?

While a reliance upon emotions as a basis of beliefs could prove reactionary, the use of reason, that is belief based upon a thorough understanding and based upon a careful assessment of the facts, could revolutionize the world. It could do so without strife or war. It could accomplish it as the result of an immutable concept: using the mind to understand the value and utility of matters of faith rather than mere blind attachment.

Through the use of reason humankind could learn to understand the various differences in the peoples of the world rather than reacting against them. People could live in peace and love rather than with hate, jealousy, and violence. Think about it. If people routinely attempted to understand their differences, what would be the result? What if they posed the question, "What can be learned from these differences?" Such an approach would certainly be superior to fear, antipathy, jealousy, animosity, misunderstanding, and/or hate. The fact is to rely upon such human emotions is catastrophic, both in personal life as well as in the growth of civilization. This is far from a condemnation of the impoverished or the unlettered. Rather, it is a basic premise. It is the premise that a true and profound understanding of God can only be achieved through the active use of the mind, that is through the use of reason.

The Soul: Proven by Science?

Obviously, humans are infused with a certain type of energy beyond the mere physical element. In each person there is a vibrancy, a type of spirit. Upon death, this spirit disappears, while the physical component remains. What's more, each person has his or her own unique compliment of this energy.

For the believer this essence is regarded as a divine gift. It is a spirit instilled within the individual by God almighty Himself. It is a gift to be used appropriately, that is in the service of God. Each human being is responsible to God for how that energy is used. That is the difference between a believer and a disbeliever. The believer uses personal or emotional powers in a positive vein, that is for the advancement of the ultimate good. In contrast, the disbeliever uses it negatively, that is for the perpetuation of hate, envy, jealousy, hostility, and greed.

Universal Energy: Its True Origin

As previously mentioned even the most simplistic of all molecules, the atom, has yet to be created. Certainly, it can be altered or corrupted. Yet, it could never be produced from scratch.

The energy system of the atom is what makes it so unique. It is also why it is impossible to reproduce. This energy system keeps it functioning, seemingly endlessly.

There is immense energy trapped in atoms. For instance, the amount of atomic energy trapped in a few grains of sand, if unleashed, could power the electricity for entire cities: for years. This is an unimaginable degree of power. Certainly, no human can make such a system. The fact is the entire human race combined could never do so. Humans are incapable of even making a grain of sand. Nor is it possible that such a power structure could develop accidentally. True, the structure of the atom can be analyzed. Yet, through science it is impossible to comprehend the source of the energy which synthesizes it and maintains its function. If all of the scientific expertise on this globe were gathered, still, it would never be able to produce an atom from nothing. Nor are the world's scientists able to explain the origin of the energy that keeps it functioning. Nor can scientists comprehend what happens to such energy upon death, when the atomic power of a living being is obviously transformed. Obviously, this energy escapes. The question is where does it go? What's more, if humans are incapable of creating it, who did?

In the living body the atom is a vital structure. What's more, through death it's vitality is dramatically altered. The atom exhibits vital energy, both in living and inanimate objects. Then, is it reasonable to presume that such an utterly refined object, which is held together by such a mind-boggling, infinitely powerful source of energy, a source which is so powerful that forcibly unleashing it leads to immediate death and destruction; could such an incredible object result from mere uncontrolled synthesis? How could such power be held within something so microscopic, so utterly tiny that even to this day no one has seen it? Certainly, this power follows a specific set of laws. What's more, it follows a purposeful system. Is it reasonable even to the slightest degree to suggest that this process, that is the synthesis of atoms, which occurs untold trillions upon trillions of times every fraction of every second, could merely occur by chance? If so, surely in an experimental environment humans could duplicate such an event, even on a small scale. Yet, the fact is regardless of the effort the creation of the atom has proven utterly elusive. Its energy source has never been determined. No one knows for certain what it even looks like. Plus, theories regarding it change constantly. The fact is the atom's exact nature is merely a matter of speculation. True, there is a certain vague understanding of the original raw materials for making atoms, which are, as far as is known, hydrogen and helium and the particles which they consist of, i.e. the electrons, protons, and neutrons. Certainly, these particles/atoms are prolific in the universe. Yet, who made the hydrogen and helium? Who synthesized the electrons, protons, and neutrons? Who developed the very concept of such particles? Who made the design that allows them to join together in perfection?

Humans are incapable of making anything from a void. This is because to create requires the input of raw energy: new energy. Humans have no means to create raw energy from nothing, yet it exists. So, Who created it?

Rather than its creators humans are energy users. They merely use or manipulate the energy already in existence. They never make it from a void. However, for those who believe, God can do this.

Thus, in the human realm regardless of how extensive the effort is, energy is impossible to synthesize from a pure void, that is from nothing. The fact is rather than being able to make energy, humans are completely dependent upon it. Thus, is it logical to assume that the all-powerful energy that drives the universe, as well as the functions of this earth, could simply and spontaneously "happen"? If not, who is making it? Think about it. Humans capture energy from various sources to drive certain functions, like the electricity that powers a city. Consider how a dam produces electrical energy. The running water, which flows over the dam, is used to spin turbines, which produce energy. This energy is transmitted through utility lines in the form of charged electrons, that is electricity, which powers homes and business.

What would happen if the dam was neglected, that is if the people operating it abandoned it? Would it still work? The fact is without constant effort, monitoring, and maintenance it would fall into disrepair and would, ultimately, malfunction. Thus, human beings produce energy from existing energy sources. They are incapable of making it from a void. They convert existing sources into power only through systematic effort. What's more, in order to generate it someone always has to be in charge. This example utterly proves that the energy of this universe could never arise from mere chance or accidents, even more so, because humans merely apply or manipulate existing energy sources, like running water, wind, or fossil fuels. With almighty God the difference is that He creates it. The fact is there must be an origin for this universal power, which drives all that exists. It is the same Being, who designed the original energy source, that is hydrogen, the substance which currently powers the universe. Thus, for instance, since specific workers are required to produce the energy to run a home or a city, there must also be an *Individual,* who generates the power that runs the vast universe. There must be a Being, Who establishes the controls required to keep the energy flowing. This must be an Individual/Being so vast, so utterly magnificent, that He defies any degree of understanding. Yet, it is even greater than this, because, besides merely generating energy, this all-powerful Being also synthesizes it: from nothing. This is the creator known as God. He is a being of an utterly unknown nature, although, assuredly, He consists of a type of energy or power that is beyond comprehension. His energy is so enormous that, singlehandedly, He created this massive universe, while retaining unlimited energy to control, guide, and, ultimately, re-create it.

Science provides evidence regarding how the universe was formed. It also suggests theories, as well as a certain amount of proof, regarding how the heavenly bodies function. Religion offers a general explanation for the purpose of this universe. It also claims directly Who operates it, something that science can only speculate about. Thus, both science and religion propose to answer some of the most fundamental questions which humans consider: What is the origin of this vast universe as well as this earth? What role do humans and other creatures play as its inhabitants? Why is there such a diversity of peoples and creatures; how did they come about? What is their precise purpose? We live and, then, ultimately, die. Then, what happens to us? Some of these questions are more important in the realm of the sciences, others to the spheres of religious thought. Yet, there is an inseparable overlap between them, since both science and religion can explain these questions on a common ground.

Science itself may be a religion to some. Yet, holding science as a way of life is far from a reason to reject the involvement of a divine power.

Frequently, those who make science their source of adoration often discover that the two coincide. James Jeans, the early 20th century astronomer, is a good example. While, originally, he failed to believe in a divine power, as his knowledge regarding the universe and the sciences increased, he recognized that a creative God must exist. The only explanation he could determine for the utterly impressive operations of the universe, that is the only rational conclusion, was that the universe was created through a specific effort by an existing power: an almighty God. Even literature written by Darwin and Huxley, major proponents of evolutionary theory, failed to refute the existence of a creative God. What's more, the modern astronomer, Stephen Hawking, concludes after thoroughly examining the cosmos that there must be a God, Who originated and controls all.

Today, scientists know that the existence of a universe without a creative force is impossible. Mathematically, the concept of a chance event leading to this organized world has been discarded. Universally, it is agreed that there is a definite force behind the origination, as well as continued development, of this universe. Who else could this be other than almighty God?

Evolution, that is the systematic alteration of species for survival, might be possible. However, it has never been proven. What's more, evolution in the form proposed by Darwin, that is by mere chance, has been thoroughly disproved. Mathematicians have demonstrated that it is virtually impossible for genes to mutate by accident to cause the needed changes in organisms. Thus, if chance fails to cause life, how did it arise? Who created the original life forms? What's more, who continues to create new or changed species? Who made the diverse species, each of which is completely unique? Who made them so independent, so utterly different, that the idea of unguided evolution seems implausible? What's more, who continues to create them? How did the most simplistic forms of life, for instance, the microbes, arise? Mathematically, their occurrence by chance has been rejected. Is there any other possibility other than the fact that all has been created by an almighty and all-controlling God?

Darwin claimed that the species developed by chance and that, apparently, an active, creative Force was unnecessary. However, as described by Gordon R. Taylor in his book, *The Great Evolution Mystery*, Darwin was wrong. Modern geneticists have proven that evolution by chance is impossible. Thus, while Darwin's ideas have been accepted virtually as fact, they are without scientific basis. Incredibly, the public is under the general impression that Darwin's work was scholarly and accurate, when, in fact, experts today regard it as faulty.

In the diversity of the species alone there is obvious evidence refuting the theory of unguided evolution. Think about it. Species are so utterly unique. For instance, consider the differences between sea life: a shark versus a sea horse, a tropical fish in contrast to a dolphin, a whale versus a clam. The differences are monumental. Is there any scientific explanation regarding how this could occur independently? In other words, could such widely divergent organisms evolve from the same primal source, strictly on their own? How could that primal source, all beginning with a few simple cells, know the blueprint for such fantastically unique creatures? Regardless of the theories he produced Darwin failed to explain such phenomena. Thus, instead of the idea of blind evolution isn't it more reasonable to presume that these are created beings, which are designed from a pre-destined mold? There is no evidence for the Darwinian system of gradual change, that is the conversion of one species to another, even for a single species. In all cases the "missing links" are lacking in the fossil record. What's more, certainly, the species are utterly different. These variations: are they anything but a testimony to the existence of an all-powerful, all-intelligent Architect, who knows in advance what the design will be?

Everything that exists adheres to systems. Thus, is it possible that the vast universe, containing untold trillions of objects, both living and non-living, could operate by a law that we, as humans, find implausible, that is the law of accident? What's more, since science is supposed to make sense or else it is rejected, then the idea that the universe could be created and recreated by mere chance is impossible to reconcile. This is because, as is proven by how everything functions on this planet, such a process is hopelessly inadequate.

Chance leads to destruction. If left to chance, systems falter and eventually involute. Thus, there is simply no possibility that the universe operates by accident. Rather, it continuously operates in perfection. Thus, through its own existence, through its obvious example, it is the opposite of chance and chaos. Since it is the opposite, this means it is highly organized. It means it is well conceived. In other words, it was and is carefully and strategically planned. It means that since its infrastructure was carefully considered, an all-powerful Intelligence, which conceived of it, must exist.

Usually, modern astronomers begin their study of the universe lacking faith in a creator. As they delve into it they usually recognize the existence of such a being. What's more, as Sir James Jeans and Stephen Hawking discovered, the universe is created with a specific, carefully developed design. Both of these modern astronomers mention the name of God as its creator.

Still, there are those who may refuse to believe in such a being. Yet, such individuals certainly believe in the authority of modern science. From a scientific point of view if the universe is chaotic, that is if it is out of control, then there is no one in charge. Or, if there was someone in charge, such a being has either abandoned His responsibility or has faltered. Yet, look at this universe as well as this very earth. Look up into the night sky. The fact is the universe never falters. What's more, it adheres to a specific system, that is it is the opposite of chaos. Assuredly, by the standards that are applied in this life someone is in charge. What other option is there?

It is easy to disbelieve in the invisible. Yet, this fails to answer the ultimate question: How did the universe, as well as this earth, originate? Furthermore, it must take great effort to maintain the function of these heavenly bodies, so who is in control? According to the astronomer James Jeans God the Creator is responsible. The conservative astronomer Stephen Hawking confirms that the universe must have originated with Him. The fact is even for those who attempt to restrict the role of God in their lives there is little conclusion other than the recognition of His incredible presence. This may explain why, when the majority of people, even those who reject His almighty role, are asked, "Who created this vast universe?", they will surely respond "God."

Chapter Three
Apes or Dignified Humans: Which is Our Origin?

Modern science is based upon the concept of the theory. A theory can never be promoted as true unless experiments prove it so. The question is do scientists truly abide by this definition? Theories are purely speculative. Again, to be valid they must be proven, specifically through well designed scientific experiments. Yet, many theories are promoted as true, even though proof is lacking. Evolution is a good example. There is some evidence that beings, even plants, evolve, that is they change, over time. Yet, no one knows for certain how this occurs. Nor does this imply that beings can develop strictly on their own by accident. No one has ever proven that even a single species has evolved gradually into another type. Scientists speculate that this might happen, but they have no proof. To date no experiments have documented such a mechanism, that is how living beings change gradually for purposes of survival. What is only known is that beings can adapt. All other concepts remain unproven.

Evolution is a fleeting concept, constantly changing

as new evidence is procured. Thus, it is not based upon facts: only unproven theories. Even as this book was going to press the theory of evolution changed once again. Now, genetic analysis indicates that the idea that humans originated in the land of apes, that is Africa, is wrong. Apparently, the original humans were a mixture of races from all over the globe. Thus, the idea, that is the theory, that humans originated in Africa directly from apes is currently under dispute. This is further evidence that any concept which is developed in science, i.e. whatever theory is devised, is only an assumption. That assumption could be justified through experiments. Yet, it may be rendered false through further findings. In other words, a concept might be regarded as true and to some degree be proven through scientific experiments. Then, another scientist performs a different experiment, perhaps more reliably, proving the idea false. The theories for the origin and destruction of the dinosaurs are excellent examples. As new evidence is procured these theories continuously change. Thus, a certain aspect of science may be strongly suspected as being accurate. However, it cannot be claimed with certainty to be true, nor can it be proved or disproved. Yet, regarding a person who believes in a creative power the issue of the true origin of the dinosaurs is simple: almighty God knows the truth about them, since He originated them and also caused their demise.

Yet, scientists can speculate, in fact, they must search for the answers, particularly if that search could prove useful to humankind. However, for those who believe in Him there is a sense of security, a type of peace, arising from the use of reason to gain a thorough understanding of God and his workings. Thus, belief in God as the Master Creator, the cause behind all events, as well as the source of all love and compassion, brings a sense of peace. In contrast, scientists are plagued continuously with uncertainty. This is especially true of those who rely on data without any conception of God's role. This is because science is so transitory, so temporary. It is continuously subject to change. What's more, a firm grip on the cause of events is ever elusive. It changes constantly, never offering even the hope of security. In contrast, as described by S. H. Pasha, Ph.D., religions are a permanent concept, a security in thought. They are impossible to refute, since they are based on the concept of belief. Religious "truths" are eternal, unlimited by time and space. As well, such truths can neither be proved or disproved, that is no one can prove that a God exists. Nor can anyone disprove His existence. Yet, as discovered incidentally by James Jeans and thousands of other scientists there is a greater degree of evidence documenting the existence of a divine power than indicating the lack of such an existence.

As mentioned previously the universe is highly organized. What's more, it remains so, continuously. In other words, nothing can disrupt it. To keep it organized power is required. Something has to generate that power. The fact is the need for such a Power

Source alone gives evidence for the existence of an almighty Master, Who controls, as well as organizes, all. Where else could this power, which is proven to exist, arise from?

Belief in the Unseen: a Religious Obligation?

Religions deal with belief in components that are imperceptible, that is things that can only be imagined. These beliefs are firmly imbedded. They cannot be forcibly changed, even with reason. In contrast, science deals with those evidences which can be perceived through the physical senses. The human being cannot see the divine being he presumes exists, nor can he fully perceive the bounties of heaven or the torments of hell. Yet, the inability to physically see an object or being is far from proof that it fails to exist. True, it is easier to believe in the obvious. For instance, if the idea of dinosaurs were presented without any evidence, i.e. without a fossil record, few people if any would believe in them.

Usually, in order to have belief in an issue there is a need to physically sense it. Humans can see and touch the bones of dinosaurs and primitive man. In the laboratory the physical characteristics of a chemical reaction can be observed, although at the molecular level the true chemical interactions are impossible to visualize. The fact is humans are incapable of physically sensing numerous scientific phenomena, like many aspects of the human nervous system, which are mere matters of theory and speculation. Modern science claims that the human nervous system is so complex that the ability to unravel its precise functions may never be achieved. For instance, the exact function of many regions of the brain remains largely unknown. Even the general function of the brain eludes scientific understanding. This is illustrated by the thinking process itself. For instance, no one knows for sure how a person accomplishes a certain function such as the thought-action of picking up a pen. Without perceiving it the thought proceeds through the brain, and then, instantaneously, it precisely happens. The pen isn't fumbled or missed. The fingers grip it exactly and proceed to write, incredibly just as fast as the brain thinks. The mechanism behind this single event is impossible to explain. Nor does anyone understand how the human being initiates what he or she wants to say and then, suddenly, it comes forth as speech. Indeed, how could a thought be instantly and miraculously transformed into spoken words? What causes that immediate reaction? How is it that, predictably, it always happens, that is humans think of what they desire to say and then, instantaneously, it is transformed into speech? The fact is the precise mechanism behind such an event is completely unknown. It is equally as much a miracle, perhaps more so, than a sudden act of God. Regarding its ability to control and guide human activities the function of the human brain is a continuous miracle.

As mentioned previously the atom, as well as its various components, that is its protons, neutrons, and electrons, has yet to be seen. Models have been constructed of its supposed appearance, Yet, no one is certain that such models are true. What is represented is purely human imagination. Thus, unseen components exist in both science and religion. Similarly, as a visible or physical creature God is beyond human senses, and so are the angels, devils, genii, spirits or any other supernatural phenomena. However, at a higher level of spiritual development humans may "sense" the existence of such beings. For such individuals the presence of these beings may become so obvious that their existence is never questioned. Yet, the fact remains they can never be seen. For instance, many people recognize the existence of angels. These angels act as guides, constantly providing subtle messages. Plausibly, each person has been assigned his or her own set. Thus, if there exist innumerable aspects of this universe that are unfathomable, how did they originate? It is true that God is imperceptible and unfathomable, that is He cannot be seen. In some circles that alone is sufficient cause to disclaim Him. Yet, this is a highly unscientific position. Think about it. Scientists are certain the atom exists. However, no one can see it or fully fathom it. In fact, its appearance is purely speculative. Yet, its existence is implicitly believed in.

The human body is a highly organized system, which functions according to deliberate laws. The same is true of the functions of the universe, as well as the earth, i.e. they all adhere to predictable and organized laws. There must be an explanation for how this degree of organization could occur. What's more, how could it happen in the universe without compromise on such a vast scale? There are tens of billions of stars in the Milky Way alone, along with untold billions of other heavenly bodies. What's more, incredibly, there are billions of Milky Ways. Yet, all these billions upon billions of objects and systems abide by definite, highly organized laws.

Regarding these billions of galaxies it is well known that they function in unison. In other words, they are all well coordinated within a specific system. Certainly, they are free of defects. What's more, their operations are predictable and organized. This is because they all abide by absolute law and order. Unlike humans, they never deviate from the universal way, which is total submission to the Higher Power. They never "resist" the need for submission. Thus, they submit fully to the authority of rule. The existence of this rule, of this absolute law and order, implies there must be a Ruler. Therefore, there must continuously be someone in charge.

Could it be otherwise? Could there be any other alternative, that is could this infinite universe possibly operate on its own? Or, is there a Massive Energy Source, Who operates all? Call Him God, Allah, Jehovah, Yahweh, the Almighty, the Master of the Universe, the Universal Force, or whatever else people deem as a description, the fact is this power is real and fully aware. What's more, when humans die, it is a power to be reckoned with.

Yet, to truly believe in God, as well as the return to Him, first relies on a component that science is unable to fully comprehend: faith in the unseen. This is the unflinching belief in a divine person, a creator and master, a Being who originated the universe and, therefore, designed all of its inhabitants. How can belief in such a creator be combined with belief in the sciences? If such a God exists, then, He would not only be the creator of the sun, but would also be the originator and designer of its very hydrogen and helium molecules. Plus, He would be the originator of the atomic reactions, which lead to the formation of these molecules. If such a God exists, then His presence doesn't even conflict with all of the components of evolutionary theory. Therefore, Cro-Magnon man would have been a part of God's creation. The missing link if any would also be His. He would be the exclusive originator of the dinosaurs. Regarding the latter rather than a product of haphazard evolution from various lower creatures He would specifically have designed each type. Each dinosaur would have been the result of a divinely-ordained mold. The fossil record appears to validate this, since there has yet to be found even a single missing link. Consider a being such as Stegosaurus. Is there even one intermediary type for it? What about Brontosaurus, now known as Apatosaurus: is there any known missing link for it? Regarding Triceratops: are there a number of well-defined interme-diaries, that is missing links, proving its evolution? Is there any other conclusion other than the fact that it is only a most glorious and great God, who is responsible?

As proof for evolution scientists claim that the hearts of reptiles possess similarities to the human heart, pointing to their common origin. Here, it makes sense that the cre-ator of both of these creatures could make molds for them which have such similarities. The genetic mechanisms, gene pools, mutations, and selection over generations supposedly alter life. Here again, this God is both aware of their presence and properly guiding their functions.

The gene is a highly organized system. Each gene is so complex that it is not even remotely possible to synthesize it. In other words, scientists are unable to duplicate it. Moreover, human experience indicates that organized systems, such as the systems involving the genes and chromosomes, as well as the entire reproductive system, would fail to develop or operate by mere chance. True, these systems may be altered by accidental or stressful events, but, like all other systems that exist on this earth, they are unable to develop merely by accident. It would require a Master of the Universe—an almighty and all-powerful Lord—to design and create such a highly organized, sophisticated, and flawless system.

Through science there is an attempt to understand existence at a molecular level. Scientists have discovered that the structure and function of organisms is systematic. They have determined that everything that exists operates with a specific purpose. What's more, they have clearly shown that everything in existence, including the most minute matter, is interconnected.

In nature widely diverse species appear to have striking similarities, both in anatomy and function. Thus, there exists a coordination in nature. These similarities and inter-connections have fueled certain aspects of the evolutionary theory, the idea being that if the heart of two uniquely different animals, such as a lizard and human, have similarities, this is proof for a direct connection. As a result, scientists claim there is no need for an all-powerful creator and that evolution operates on its own. In other words, they believe that somehow the universe created life independently. Furthermore, they claim that such similarities prove that all that exists originated from a single source through spontaneous evolution.

A careful analysis proves this reasoning to be flawed. Rather than retaining similarities uncontrolled evolution would lead to mass chaos. Thus, over the eons similarities would be diminished, perhaps obliterated. The fact that despite the passing of billions of years there exist similarities in the "molds" for various creatures indicates the oneness of nature. It confirms the existence of a pervasive design. Evolutionists claim all creatures have one source in common. H. T. Bray in his book, *The Living Universe*, claims that the universe is indivisibly one. Yet, incredibly, this very claim, this oneness of nature, as well as the oneness of the vast universe, lends a greater degree of proof for the existence of an all-powerful and almighty Lord than for the evolutionary theory. In other words, it gives evidence for the existence of a singular source for all. The similarities between species may serve as clear signs, which enforce the possibility of the existence of a divine controller and coordinator. What's more, someone had to conceive of and, ultimately, design the various creatures. Someone had to be responsible for organizing the creative event. Someone had to make the molds. That same One then had to alter the molds to establish the various species. In other words, He had to in a timely fashion create new species, as evolution dictated. What's more, this same Being must keep such a complex system in order. Herein, the concept is simple: blind evolution without an organizing and controlling force is impossible.

Chance Event or Via Almighty God—Which is the Mechanism?

The fact that living creatures adapt to their environments is undeniable. If this is the definition of evolution, then there is a degree of truth to it. In other words, creatures possess the ability to adapt to various stresses. This means they have an inherent intelligence. Yet, evolution itself is precisely the opposite of chance. This adaptation follows a specific system, largely based upon genetics. In fact, it is a deliberate system necessary for survival. Evolution, which may be defined as the alteration of living beings over the course of time for the purposes of survival, serves a critical purpose. Because it serves such a purpose, it fails to meet the definition of "chance" or "accidental." Thus, by definition it is a controlled and purposeful event. The fact that it is controlled implies that it must be guided. This makes sense, since all that exists in the human realm requires guidance. For instance, to control a missile it must be guided. Without a well designed and intricately functioning guidance system, it would fail. Thus, it is no surprise that for the infinitely more complex human beings guidance is required. In fact, the mechanisms behind their development and/or evolution are intricately related to certain biological laws. Without the preordained existence of such laws, evolution would fail to occur. The question is, Who is guiding it and Who made the biological laws that it is based upon? The fact is if such laws failed to exist all would be annihilated. It is agreed that such universal laws exist. Yet, who is the Law-Maker? Scientists may imply that an all-involved being is unimportant or perhaps doesn't even exist. Yet, all scientists admit that for laws to be enacted in this life a law-maker is required. For instance, men make laws for ruling nations. In other words, humans recognize the existence of law-makers on earth. What about the rule of this vast universe? Sensibly, it too must be ruled by a law-maker.

The theory that evolution, that is specific changes in the species, occurs purely randomly fails to withstand scientific scrutiny. This is because such a concept violates the operations of this universe as well as the earth. It is because the universe adheres to a specific highly organized system, not the chaos that would be expected from uncontrolled or accidental events.

The issue is that in science a specific view or agenda is promoted. Scientists claim that the universe developed solely by accident. In other words, it developed without an Ever-Present God. Furthermore, they claim that it evolved completely on its own, without Him. According to this view there is no requirement for a controlling and involved God, since the universe evolves by itself. All events simply happen: there is no active Force. Thus, by this thinking accidental evolution alone is sufficient to explain the universe's operations. It has its own power source, which happened on its own without anyone generating or controlling it. Regarding such a view the point is where is the proof?

The word accident itself connotes only one possibility: disaster. According to *Webster's Dictionary* an accident is "an event that occurs *without one's expectation, an undesigned sudden or unexpected happening.*" It is also defined as a "mishap," an "unfortunate event, a disaster, or a casualty." Other synonyms used to define it include hazard, misfortune, calamity, and possibility. Of note in the aforementioned definition is the italicized section (my italics), "without one's expectations." This implies that anything which happens accidentally is unplanned, that is it lacks a specific design. Yet, hundreds of modern astronomers, such as Stephen Hawking and George Smoot, claim that everything that exists in the vast universe, as well as the earth itself, follows a specific plan. Rather than merely evolving the fact is this universe functions via a system that is completely predictable. It is as if it has been carefully pre-planned. In other words, evidence for uncontrolled evolution is nil. Therefore, there must be a controlling Force. In fact, such a force must be an actual "physical" being. With this *scientific model* there is no margin for unplanned or chaotic events. In other words, someone must be in absolute control of the universe as well as the earth. True, an understanding of the exact nature of such a force is lacking. Yet, what is certain is that it exists, because all that exists is under a mighty control. The fact is this being exerts control even over every human, from birth to death. Yet, this Authority is also in complete control of the final phase, that is the transportation of the living essence to its ultimate destination. It is the essence found in every being, that is the living soul, which survives death. Modern science has proven that this subtle energy exists. Its nature is unfathomable, but, like the almighty Master, the fact that it exists is indisputable. Precisely how or where it is transported remains unknown. Yet, the fact that it exists and that it escapes upon death is indisputable.

It is obvious that the structure of this world, as well as the universe, is highly organized. In daily life it takes effort to organize even minimal projects, such as making a meal, planning a vacation, performing an exercise routine, etc. Certainly, organizing and performing a well-designed scientific experiment takes significant effort. In contrast, the degree of effort which is required to organize and operate heavenly bodies—billions of them—is unimaginable. To reiterate, to conduct experiments human effort is required. Without the human element, that is the efforts of living, thinking creatures, experiments would be impossible. No computer can on its own conduct them. There must always be a human administrator. Logically, the universal experiment, that is the constant creation and evolution of the uncountable heavenly, as well as living, bodies, also requires an Experimenter. If the need for an experimenter is admitted in any earthly project, why deny it for the vast universe? Any such denial is tantamount to outright bias, in fact, hypocrisy.

Science is supposedly unbiased. It is promoted as neutral, never political. For scientists, to show bias is highly unprofessional. They fear being associated with it. In fact, such an association would be catastrophic, because their careers would be destroyed. Yet, scientists clearly demonstrate bias towards a divine being. If they were truly unbiased, they would at a minimum remain neutral. For instance, regarding a divine power if they were neutral, their language, that is the positions they popularize, would demonstrate it. In other words, at least they would never dissuade people from what is truly evident. In this instance since it is beyond question scientists might admit that the universe is under a mighty control. They might qualify this by stating that the exact nature of this control is unknown. This would be merely stating the obvious facts. This is because as all astronomers agree no one precisely understands this controlling force, but the fact is it definitely exists. Because of the obvious facts they would also admit that rather than there being numerous divine beings, such as the ethereal claim of the existence of "the gods," this force is One. In other words, rather than the existence of numerous divinities scientific evidence points to a Oneness of this universe. What's more, they would attest to the fact that matter could never develop on its own and that behind it there is a Source. Yet, far from remaining neutral scientists clearly promote the concept of the lack of an intensively involved divine being. Even so, if a person thinks about it, in other words, if he carefully uses his innate reasoning powers, it becomes obvious that there is someone in control. Human concepts or perceptions of time may fail to fathom it, yet that is no justification for refuting it. As well, it becomes clear that such a force is alive and fully in command. Evidence for chaos in the universe is lacking. Rather, everywhere it adheres to a mighty order. Everywhere its operations are predictable.

The universe follows an incredibly precise control. This lends proof for the existence of a controlling force, which is constantly maintaining, monitoring, and managing it. In other words, from a scientific point of view the universe there is a definite force keeping it organized. Such a concept is based upon reason. Can scientists offer a reasonable argument to counter it? If not, why make the claim about anything other than what is obvious?

The universe is the epitome of exactness. It is also utterly predictable. Furthermore, it is completely dependable. This means it follows a pre-arranged plan. For a plan to exist there must be a Planner. The fact is its degree of organization is so grand that it is incomprehensible. This unfathomable system: wouldn't it make sense that there exists as its source a single power so mighty that He singlehandedly operates it? What's more, one such being is obviously sufficient, in fact, required. If there were several Gods, that is several ultimate authorities, this would pose an insurmountable dilemma. This is because, clearly, as is demonstrated by experience in this life such beings would fail to cooperate. The fact is they would be competing against each other, rather, fighting each other. Is there any other possibility?

The greatness of this design is easy to understand. Simply look at the star-laden sky. Is there a descrition other than the fact that it is utterly elegant and magnificent? Plus, it is monumentally vast, beyond anything humans can conceive. All that humans can perceive is a minuscule portion. A single galaxy, containing billions of stars, is beyond imagination. Yet, there are billions of them, with trillions upon trillions of stars, planets, moons, and infinitely more. Such a vast system could never arise or operate haphazardly. The fact is the idea of accidental or unguided existence defies any degree of common sense.

Humans function through systems and laws. Animals abide by certain laws, for instance, the self-protective instinct, which guides their every action. In biology it is known that animals function in utter perfection, as if they are directly guided. Is it different for the billions of galactic systems? Scientists may claim that the universal systems operate without the direct hand of God. Yet, not a single aspect of their existence supports such a theory. The point is if the universe is an accident, is there any proof? Is there even the most minute degree of scientific evidence, which supports accidental creation? For those who maintain that the universe operates by chance are there even any plausible theories? If so, are there any reasonable examples or experiments to support such theories? In other words, in all the observations made by modern science is there even the slightest degree of evidence, which proves that the world functions independently, that is without the direct control of a supreme being? Why make the claim without evidence, that is if the basis of such a claim is supposedly scientific? Or, is it that people simply wish to argue about the existence of God?

The universe is predictable. Therefore, it is reasonable to presume that there exists a force, which makes it dependable and which keeps it from self-destructing. It is a Force which maintains law and order. It is a Force which is involved in every aspect of this universe, including our very lives.

Scientists understand that the universe is designed in perfection. Yet, is it reasonable that while this degree of perfection, this incomprehensibly sophisticated design, is agreed upon, the existence of a designer is disputed? Rationally, if the design is accepted, then so must be the existence of the One who designed it. This is how people operate in this life. For instance, no one buys designer clothes or other objects, such as jewelry and furniture, while rejecting or arguing against the designer. In fact, usually, people praise the designer for his/her effort. Regarding the designer of the universe is He ever recognized or praised for it? Is He routinely honored? In some circles is He even recognized to exist? This is worth serious consideration, that is for those willing to give it thought.

Consider the objects or beings which exist in this world. Is it reasonable to presume that the efficient and well organized atom or molecule: could it truly develop by accident? Could it only develop through unguided evolution? Regarding the human body could it, with its exceptionally intricate nature, develop without a designer? Could it simply arise on its own, for instance, from apes? What about the human brain, with its immeasurable complexity? It has a structure and function which is so complex that it is impossible to map. Could such a highly intricate and complex system evolve merely by accident? Or, is it conceivable that a Power exists, which utterly creates it plus guides it?

Humans are merely observers and experimenters. They can collect data. At best they may manipulate the environment about them. Yet, they are unable to create, from literally nothing, from mere dust, earth, or mineral matter, or anything else, any kind of molecular raw material, the raw material that is the basis of existence. Humans are certainly capable of utilizing the existing matter or raw material and can produce objects from it. However, all such objects are inanimate, that is non-living. For example, humans can make cars, airplanes, trains, living quarters, furniture, and much more. Yet, they are incapable of creating even a single living thing. Despite great advances in technology this has yet to happen. Thus, even with all the most fantastic human achievements the creation of life or even the building blocks thereof, such as genetic material, the very material which makes every living creature, even every plant, in fact, every blade of grass, unique, has proven impossible.

Scientists have been unable to create even the most basic molecules, for instance, molecules of sodium, potassium, and calcium. Such molecules are obviously divinely created. No human can produce them. What's more, no one knows how they arose. There are hundreds of molecules and substances in this earth, all of which are useful to humankind. Yet, the most that humans can achieve is to use and/or manipulate the existing raw materials. For example, if a raw material on this earth is utterly exhausted or destroyed—water, oil, natural gas, minerals, or oxygen—who would replace it? Is there anyone other than God?

Humans extract from the earth minerals and metals. Then, they use these substances to produce the necessary inventions. Yet, are they capable of creating them? Even though minerals are the most basic components in existence, it is well known that such molecules are the epitome of systematic organization. The origin of and mechanisms behind their refined, electrical, and/or crystalline structures defy all comprehension. Yet, who organizes them? What power synthesizes them? Who produces their crystalline structure, their wavelengths, and their specific functions? Who made the enzymes into which these molecules fit so perfectly? Is it chaos? The fact is it is inconceivable that the perfection seen in nature could happen on its own. *Webster's Dictionary* defines an accident as a disaster. The universe is simply too perfect to meet this definition.

Rather than chaos the universe, as well as the earth, operates via utter precision. Everything in existence appears to function in perfection. No one completely understands how this happens. This degree of organization is easy to see: the way birds fly seemingly effortlessly, the way fish swim, remaining buoyant, how humans rhythmically walk and run: it all works so perfectly and dependably. However, this degree of organization also occurs on the microscopic, that is molecular, level. A good example is how specific natural molecules interact with human cells. For instance, enzymes, minerals, vitamins, and various other biologically active molecules function according to specific systems. Incredibly, each molecule has its own site within or on the cells, where it attaches. These sites are known as receptors. When these molecules attach to these receptors, certain biological reactions are stimulated. The fact is enzymes and minerals fit perfectly into their receptors. The point is a fit of exactness must be pre-designed.

Humans are incapable of performing such a feat. For instance, pharmaceutical manufacturers attempt to produce medicines which fit into certain receptors. Yet, they never fit perfectly. Rather, they, in essence, obstruct the receptor site. This is why they cause side effects. They interfere with normal function. In fact, drugs may readily damage receptors, causing permanent harm—even death. Thus, in biology the perfection of the aforementioned degree—the exact fit—must result from a superhuman degree of design. The fact is it must have as its designer an unfathomable, infinitely powerful Source, that power we call God.

Space modules are an excellent example of the need for perfection. Space stations and satellites have on their exteriors certain receptors into which tools, modules, or other devices attach. For the engineers who design them it takes great effort to perfect the fit. The slightest error could lead to catastrophe. This is certainly exemplified by the recent space shuttle debacle. Here, a slight defect

led to utter death and destruction. The point is for critical issues humans must make an enormous effort to
ensure perfection. The slightest error or degree of neglect could result in utter catastrophe. Could it be any different for the uncountable relationships that exist in
nature and in the vast universe? If humans must work
carefully and arduously here, a similar effort would be
required to keep the universe in perfection. Thus, Who
engineers the interrelationships in living beings, that is
the molecule-receptor function, of insulin, vitamins,
minerals, estrogen, testosterone, cortisone, enzymes, and
untold thousands of other biological substances? Who
keeps it all working as an organized system? Who creates the exact fit? Is it any other than God? All of these
substances function via a highly specific mechanism,
that is by attaching to specific receptors. The receptors
are found mainly on the outside of cells, but they may
also be found inside them, for instance, on or in the
nucleus. The fit must be perfect, otherwise disaster, that
is cell damage or death, results. There is another unique
mechanism, which would appear to be highly planned.
Each molecule has its own unique energy. Incredibly,
this energy is the same as exhibited by the receptor site.
In other words, the molecule and its receiver, i.e. its
receptor, generate the same signal. Essentially, for every
molecule there is a sort of microscopic homing device.
This is a type of energy or perhaps chemical process. It
is an energy which directs it to destination, that is its
receptor site. Thus, the molecule and receptor are perfectly suited. Chance could have never resulted in such a

perfect energy match, nor could mindless evolution. With the perfect fit the proper biological reaction is initiated, and the result is cellular activation. The perfect fit implies there is order in the function of organisms, and this is precisely how biological beings operate. What a proof this is, what a scientific fact, that the beings in this world could never have developed spontaneously. Thus, if the laws of science are used as the determinant, these specialized features, that is this perfect fit, could only have developed as a result of a specific plan, which is preordained. As mentioned previously Webster's defines an accident as a mishap: an undesigned event. Undesigned implies unplanned. It means, essentially, out of control. This is precisely the opposite of how living beings operate. It is the opposite of how everything else in existence, including the heavenly bodies, functions. The fact is whatever exists on this earth, as well as within the universe, operates with a specific direction and under a definite design. Thus, by this modern world's own definition there is no possibility that the beings in this universe, as well as non-living objects, such as mineral matter and heavenly bodies, could have developed accidentally. Rather, as is indicated by the definition in the dictionary the operations of the universe are precisely the opposite of an accident. Thus, it is the antonym, that is the opposite, which more correctly describes the nature of this universe. The antonyms for accident include plan, certainty, intention, precise law, calculation, purpose, and preparation. To make a plan a Planner is required, to establish certainty an all-knowing, all-aware One is needed, to devise a perpetual and well-prepared design a methodical Creator is required, to establish precise laws an exacting Law-Giver is needed, to make accurate, dependable calculations a Master Mathematician is necessary, and to prepare with a purpose an organized Preparer is required. Thus, by the modern world's own definitions there exists a Law-Creating and Law-Giving God.

Humans possess vast abilities. The human mind can invent and create, that is it can produce from raw materials things never before conceived. Through the creativeness of human inventions modern society has risen to great heights. The mind has proven to be a powerful faculty, responsible for creating both what is useful for humankind as well as what will eventually lead to its doom. Yet, this mind of ours: how did it originate? That complex nervous system, which is coordinated to such a mind-boggling extent that it allows humans to invent the unknown: is the development of such an unfathomable degree of complexity merely the consequence of unguided events, mere chance? Or, is the mind-power which gives human beings untold creative abilities, in fact, synthesized by a Power infinitely greater than anything which can be conceived?

Science has proven incapable of determining the precise structure and function of the brain. Even basic issues, such as how thought is generated, remain unknown. Regarding the intricacies of the brain, even if all of the neurological specialists in the world were called forth to study it, such a team would fail to completely or even remotely understand it. Therefore, what else could explain its existence besides the fact that it is created by an infinitely intelligent creative power?

The brain is highly sophisticated. Its capacity to operate is utterly beyond human understanding. Evolution itself is insufficient to explain its development. The brain is so complex that its functions largely evade scientific understanding. These interconnections are too complex to have developed without special guidelines. In other words, a specialized pre-ordained blueprint was required. Thus, is it conceivable that such a complex, sophisticated organ could develop by chance?

Humankind is the epitome of creation. Yet, are humans able to build even the slightest fertile germ seed? It is not for a lack of trying. Through untold thousands of experiments scientists have attempted to create the components of life and, with the exception of a few non-viable amino acids, have thoroughly failed. For instance, even the most simplistic type of genetic material, a mere chromosome, is impossible to create. What's more, incredibly, humans are incapable of even making a single plant seed. How could they? They cannot be entirely certain regarding its composition. Furthermore, the creation of an animal cell has proven utterly elusive. In fact, there is not even the most remote chance that humans will be able to do so. Think about it. Even if every human mind, that is every top scientist, were gathered, can such a team produce life from nothing? Can even the raw materials be created, the matter—mere molecules—needed to produce creation? Then, what of an original being: a species? Regardless of how vast the effort it is all utterly elusive.

Humans are incapable of creating. Rather, they are only capable of manipulating, that is altering, existing creation. The fact is they are themselves created beings.

There is no conflict between belief in God and belief in the sciences. In fact, the concept of a divinity is compatible with the majority of scientific theories. Islam, for one, fails to argue against any of these principles. Thus, the Big Bang did likely occur. The Primeval Soup probably did exist. That Soup certainly originated much of life as we know it. To refute this violates both reason and established evidence. Thus, the question is does it make sense that all of these phenomena could occur entirely on their own, with no one to oversee, guide, and control events? That Bang: could it possibly have happened in utter chaos, without an ever-present guiding force? Who intentionally planned its mechanism and caused it to evolve in a specific direction? Who initiated it? Yet, regarding the consequences of that Bang could it have developed on its own into this monumentally vast universe, with its intensive degree of precision and organization? Could vast planets, complete with the necessary moons and suns, as well as their various and magnificent land structures, oceans, and atmospheres, have originated without a specific plan, that is without a guiding Force? Regarding these uncountable planets, each is operating in a spectacular, elegant, and systematic fashion. Who is in control of them? Each is functioning without even the slightest glitch or error. Each is powered by a Force, which humans are unable to perceive. What's more, each follows its own set of rules, adhering to a pre-ordained lifespan. Humans may fail to understand the exact nature of the forces behind them. Even by the top scholars the physics and mathematics responsible for their operation are only minimally understood. Yet, what is undeniable is that there exists an all-powerful control. It may be impossible to perceive it, however, it exists.

Can anything that we know of become organized by accident? Think about it. If you believe it is so, provide even a single example. Consider this earthly life. Does anything accidentally become organized? For instance, can the top of a person's desk become organized by chance, or does someone have to make the effort? Does a home become organized on its own, or must energy be put into it? Can a garden or lawn become orderly without assistance, or must someone do the work? The fact is an effort is constantly required to create organization. In contrast, a lack of effort results in disorganization. Regarding a garden if no one tends to it, what happens? It turns wild and, ultimately, bears little fruit. The same happens with a lawn. In other words, without a constant and systematic effort disorganization, that is chaos, results.

In this existence everything of any consequence must be managed. In other words, someone must be in control. This is because a controlling force is required to coordinate events, that is to make events or processes function smoothly. The lack of such a coordinator undermines the efficiency of an organization or project, leading to failure. Without a coordinator nothing constructive happens. If this is the case here, could it be any different for the vast universe? Would the complex biological˚ systems of the human body, that is the cells and organs, follow anything but the same concept, that is to be under an almighty Control? In other words, if there is a dispute regarding the involvement of God in this world or in our very bodies, how strong is the evidence? Can scientific evidence prove that the early primeval soup spontaneously gave rise to man? Can it demonstrate that this was an uncontrolled or chance event? Is there firm evidence of a direct link between apes and humans? In other words, has the missing link clearly been found? The fact is there is no known missing link. Rather, apes and humans remain distinct species. What's more, even if science provides evidence for chance events or evolution, does this negate the role of a creator in such a process?

Yet, regarding the past human beings can only speculate, that is theorize. The human mind fails to understand for certain how life developed and/or evolved. What is known is that this universe is under an impressive and dominating control. It is also known that human beings have no power over it. What happens throughout the vast universe is strictly under the domain of a higher power, which is infinitely more powerful than anything imaginable. The same is true of the earth. If the climate changes, that is out of human control. If the sun diminishes in intensity, affecting our very existence, there is no means to boost it. If an asteroid or comet hurtles down to the earth, it cannot be stopped. Nor is it possible for human beings to alter their ultimate destiny, that is how long they will live or when and even where they will die. The fact is all the serious events, such as life and death, as well as the ultimate destiny, are beyond human control. What's more, when human beings die, there will be a transition. That transition is a type of evolution, one under the control of a Mighty Force beyond human comprehension.

Scientists know that beyond the physical body there exists a substance, a type of essence. It is an essence which is unique to each individual. It exists in every living being. Upon death that essence disappears. With the death of a loved one or even a dear pet it becomes utterly obvious. When death occurs, that essence, which weighs some seven ounces, disappears, rather, is transformed. No one knows for sure where it goes. Yet, its existence is certain. Yet, it is transported, that is it is removed to a dimension beyond human understanding.

Evolution or Divine Systems—Which is the Source?

Is there any evidence for modern science's claim that evolution happens on its own? Is there any firm reason to believe that it develops without an overriding and predestined force? The view that evolution is its own force fails to solve the most fundamental issue, which is Who created the evolving universe? Who initiated it? Who made its design? Who gave it the Laws by which it operates? What mechanism or force keeps it organized? What's more, Who created the biological systems that allow beings to evolve? Furthermore, Who created the life-force within all creatures, that substance usually described as the soul? The soul is eternal. Everything else—everything physical—fades. Who created that spirit, which exists in all animals and humans, and which escapes upon their deaths? Who originated the laws, that is the various physical systems, by which this universe operates? The Islamic view is whatever has happened throughout the untold eons of time to the earth and its various inhabitants, these occurrences have been established and governed upon by a God, a Master of unfathomable powers, a Being who alone has the capacity to control all that exists within this vast universe. What's more, as originally described by S. H. Pasha He is not merely God the Creator. Rather, He is actively involved, constantly altering and controlling His system. Rather, He is a God who creates and also re-creates. He is also a God who is in communication with the very essence of human existence, that is human souls.

Evolution is mentioned merely because of how it is viewed by scientists. The popular thinking is that since creatures evolve and since evolution, i.e. the ability of species to adapt to changing environments, can to some degree be documented, therefore, there is no God. Beings supposedly evolve on their own. There is nothing which creates or organizes that evolution, that is it simply happens by chance. Yet, this view fails to explain the most fundamental issue, that is Who created the foundations of life? Who synthesized the building

blocks of biological existence, which are so deliberately organized, so refined and sophisticated that they bog-
gle the mind? Who created the intricate and precise
strands of DNA and RNA, which are so utterly complex
that they are impossible to duplicate? According to the
Scientific American the DNA and RNA are "highly
structured" beyond anything imaginable. Could such
precision-oriented molecules have spliced themselves
together on their own? Could they have become so
utterly organized merely by haphazard evolution?
Mathematically, this is impossible. The fact is it would
take an enormous amount of time—longer than the existence of the earth—billions, in fact, tens of billions of
years, for even a single strand of DNA to develop accidentally, let alone an organism. Thus, the odds are completely against it. Beings or even their basic components, such as cellular machinery or genetic material,
simply fail to become designed on their own. Consider
intensively complex structures, like genetic material,
which is itself alive. Consider even a mere component
of the cell such as the factory-like mitochondrion. These
are highly complex structures, the function of which is
little understood. Could even these develop on their
own? The fact is these are simply too complex to arise
by accident. In other words, chance development of a
highly organized and complex molecule, such as DNA,
or a cellular factory, such as the mitochondrion, is mathematically impossible. Without a specific known blueprint it would be impossible to evolve to such perfection. The existence of such a blueprint demonstrates the

need for a Master Architect. In other words, the final conclusion—the scientific analysis—is that all must have been specifically designed. Thus, for biological molecules, let alone independent species, a living designer is required. Rather than evolution as the source is this anything but ultimate proof for the presence of an active creator, a designer of all? Here, it is worthy to note that the definitions in *Webster's Dictionary* clearly indicate that accidental or chance events never lead to organization and certainly never induce the degree of organization seen in genetic material. There are untold millions of types of DNA and RNA, all with their own unique structures. The indication is that all these unique types were pre-planned. Only a singularly powerful divine being could develop such designs. What's more, these designs are highly organized. They are not the bizarre or mutated forms, which would be expected from blind evolution. Therefore, there is a singular source for their origin. What's more, the scientific record proves that species originate suddenly and disappear suddenly, not offering nearly enough time for gradual evolution. This fully disputes the theory of unguided and/or spontaneous evolution.

The concepts used to support evolution are vague. Little or no scientific evidence is provided to prove that beings are gradually converted into different species. A good example is the idea that apes evolved into humans. All that has been discovered are unique species of humans and unusual species of apes. However, the confirmation for direct evolution is lacking. In other words, the missing link has yet to be discovered. Humans and apes remain two distinct species. Even the fossils deemed missing links are entirely different species. Thus, Who created, organized, and segregated the various beings into their different types? What's more, Who created, rather, continues to create, the infinite range of species? Furthermore, Who synthesizes the genetic code, which is unique to each species? True, such species may evolve in a way that is somewhat predictable, yet, how did they originate? Who designed their uniqueness? Every creature has its own special attributes, all designed to perfection. Is it reasonable to believe that various creatures, that is the tens of millions of species, developed exclusively by accident? The fact is mathematically not even a single one could have done so. Thus, how did they arise?

Science and Religion: Are they Compatible?

In North America science and religion have become virtually polarized. Yet, they can work in unison. Common goals, such as the advancement of civilization, can be realized. Unfortunately, today, with science one of the obstacles is that it is largely controlled by business interests, especially in regard to finance. The fact is within scientific circles bias is extensive. The fact is this bias is so extensive that human benefit is often placed secondary. In other words, the research is often biased toward financial interests rather than the service of humankind. Thus, it lacks the independence necessary to fully benefit the human race.

To religious people science is dysfunctional, largely because of its refusal to accept the creative God. In contrast, scientists claim that religion is unscientific, because it is based strictly upon belief, without supportive evidence. Thus, catastrophically, there is lacking a universal way of thinking which binds these disciplines. What's more, in science financial interests are usually the motivation rather than altruism. A cooperative approach can only occur if both science and religion adopt the same concepts of belief, that is the same principles for improving this world, both for its inhabitants and the earth itself.

In religion people believe in the unknown. In contrast, in modern science proof is demanded before beliefs or theories are accepted. In this regard lab experiments are incapable of proving the physical presence of God. Perhaps His presence might be sensed, however, He can never physically be seen. For this reason many scientists are embarrassed to discuss or consider the possibility of an almighty though technically invisible God. This embarrassment or reticence may partially be due to fear of reproach from colleagues, who, in respect to a creative God, are adamant regarding the need for proof. The fact is scientists often posture in favor of disbelief, even though, privately, they believe in Him.

This attitude is largely because in science whatever exists must be strictly defined, whereas in religion beliefs are impossible to define. As described by S. H. Pasha science is basically a single principle, with definitions common to all its divisions. Religion, with its many forms and outgrowths, is based on a variety of principles, none of which can be scientifically proven.

Many religious systems exist, some of which may have, at times, opposed the advancement of science. For instance, during the early Christian era scientists were routinely persecuted. Even famous men, such as Galileo and Copernicus, encountered resistance. In fact, such men were persecuted when trying to present the proofs of science. Unfortunately, in the scientific community this practice continues today, especially when discoveries threaten vested interests. Yet, there is one "religion"—one way of thinking—which historically aided the growth of the sciences, in fact, invented them. This is the religion of Islam.

Chapter Four

Islam: Its Origins and Achievements

Islam encourages the advancement of science. The world's top historians, such as Gibbon, Toynbee, Sarton, Renan, Goldstein, Welty, Hill, Turner, Wells, Briffault, and Durant, have shown that the very roots of modern science belong with the early Islamic civilization. Durant states that the creation of algebra and chemistry was due to the efforts of this early Islamic culture. The Islamic achievements in astronomy, medicine, pharmacology, geography, geology, physics, zoology, and botany are innumerable, well recorded, and highly advanced for their time. What's more, Islam was directly responsible for the development of European science and achievements. For example, Columbus received his notion that the world was round from studying in an Islamic university.

Islam arose among the sixth/seventh century Arabs. These Arabs were largely an illiterate people, who worshiped idols. Immersed in every conceivable evil, the Arabs were typical of the barbarians of that era. They had no interest in refinement or the sciences. They were crude and hedonistic. Were it not for Islam they would have remained so, perhaps forever. Thus, for the people of Arabia, as well as the entire Middle East, only Islam created a true, refined civilization. Islam is far from an element of the past. In increasing numbers people are attracted to it, because it creates personal and social change. In contrast, any other way which the Arabs or other Middle Eastern peoples historically adopted, such as paganism, idol worship, and autocratic rule, utterly failed them. Certainly, they proved incapable of producing even a single civilized society, where people of all cultures and races could interact together. Even today, clamoring for the 'Arab' banner has proven faulty. The typical ideologies still popular in these regions today, such as Arab nationalism, have never created social change. Rather, nationalism or tribal attachment merely perpetuates civilization's decline. Islam alone creates the change required for human advancement. It alone elevates the human state, infusing it with sublime goals. Only it revolutionizes human society, causing the positive results, which advance the human condition. It exclusively brings peace, happiness, and the love of humanity to a world consumed by misery, strife, torment, and despair. This is why people throughout the world are seeking Islam as a way of life. They realize that it is the only way of life which offers such benefits.

The Arab condition was revolutionized by a single event: the revelation of the Qur'an to the Prophet Muhammad. It was this event alone which catapulted the Arabs from a life of barbarism to the greatest heights of civilization. The fact is the Qur'an was the direct source for the advancement of civilization, whether Eastern and Western. With its first revealed word, that is, "Read (i.e. use your reasoning abilities, which are naturally existent within the brain)," the Qur'anic revolution began like no other. The use of the intellect was preached, while intolerance, barbarism, corruption, and violence were shunned. Within 23 years the Muslims developed the beginnings of the most law-abiding, sophisticated civilization ever known. Ultimately, people became Muslims in droves, abandoning their errant and barbaric ways. Only the most upright and elegant of behaviors were adopted. Within 200 years the followers of Islam surpassed any degree of advancement accomplished by the ancients, far exceeding them in literary and, particularly, scientific output. According to Thomas Goldstein Islam created the modern sciences, which led to the creation of modern civilization.

It could only be Islam which created the sciences. This is because in the Islamic civilization the credo was to read, study, teach, and think. It was the Prophet Muhammad who said "Search for knowledge to the furthest reaches of the globe (i.e. even to China)." The fact is he was the first to urge the masses to become intellectually inclined. In contrast, in Europe the seeking of knowledge was regarded as a crime.

This approach to learning encompassed all peoples, not just "believers." It was certainly true both for intellectuals and common citizens. Robert Briffault in his book, *Rational Evolution*, claims that during the Islamic Era only learning distinguished one person from another: race and religion had no impact.

No other civilization either prior or since has maintained such a system. As originally described by S. H. Pasha it was the first society ever to institute public education, the impact of which is still felt today. Thus, for both scholars and everyday people civilization was perfected through the use of reason and the authority of the book.

Islam created scientific advancement, while mentioning the name of God. Books on the sciences were dedicated in His name. What's more, credit was given to Him throughout. Thus, Islam was the original, in fact, the only, system which promoted the worship of God simultaneously with the creation of science. For the first time in history the name of God was recognized and glorified during the intellectual process as well as during the performance of detailed scientific experiments.

Because of its emphasis on using the powers of reason, as well as the storehouse of knowledge it produced, Islam singlehandedly eradicated barbarism in Arabia as well as in the rest of the Middle East. Central Asia was completely rejuvenated, as was Persia. North Africa became enlightened, as did Spain, Sicily, parts of France, and southern Italy. Meanwhile, the European continent was slow to adopt its brilliance. This was because it was held deeply in check by the Church, with seemingly no hope of recovery. Bigoted church practices stymied, rather, reversed, progress. Yet, ultimately, Islam overcame the darkness of Europe, seeding it, in fact, spoon-feeding it, with the intellectual light that it required for its resurrection. The fact is the intellectual revolution it created was so intense that its repercussions are extensively felt today.

Think about it. How did the terminology, Arabic numerals, arise? What is the origin of words such as sodium, sofa, satin, handkerchief, sash, coffee, mocha, spinach, apricot, artichoke, alfalfa, apricot, sugar, luffa, lilac, retina, menninges, drug, jar, borax, boron, coral, carat, algebra, arithmetic, average, zero, logarithm, sine, cosine, tangent, admiral, almanac, Almagest, alkali, alcohol, and aldehyde plus hundreds of others (notice the "al" at the beginning of many of these words)? They all originated from Arabic.

In contrast to the antagonistic attitude in medieval Europe Western historians describe how Islam lacked hostility towards the sciences. In fact, it was the sciences' benefactor in the most phenomenal way. Here is an interesting example. After conquering the seventh century's dilapidated civilizations the Muslims began mixing with other cultures. There, they encountered the manuscripts of the ancients. These manuscripts were, of course, in foreign languages. It was S. H. Pasha who first described how the Muslim Caliphs offered translators a tempting incentive. Upon completion of their manuscripts translators received the weight of the book in gold.

The offer of the equivalent of gold weight was a monumental incentive. As a result of this method the translators of Islam produced vast volumes far greater than any previous civilization. Singlehandedly, through its efforts the knowledge of the ancients was preserved for all times to come.

For the first time in history divine inspiration assisted, rather, motivated, scientific achievement. Muslims of all types, black, white, and yellow, Middle Eastern, African, Asian, and European, regarded the pursuit of the sciences as such a strict obligation that the failure to do so was viewed as an offense. Thus, ignorance was regarded as the antithesis of Islam. So was and is bias towards specific races. In other words, Islam is completely opposed to the idea that certain races are intellectually superior.

While in the past the learned civilizations kept their knowledge in the charge of the elite, Islam regarded and, in fact, still regards, learning as a divine obligation: for everyone. What's more, in contrast to ancient Greece, where outsiders were discriminated against or enslaved, the environment of Islam provided equal status for all races. Thus, as compared to all previous civilizations the Islamic one was the most tolerant. In fact, its liberal approach remains unmatched even to this day. People of all cultures, tribes, races, and religions studied together without discrimination. Incredibly, no one was belittled because of race, color, or creed. Even former slaves became refined scholars. It was Islamic civilization which produced the scholarly al-Jaahiz. A former African (black) slave, he is today regarded as perhaps the greatest literary genius of all time. Al-Jaahiz produced nearly 200 books, all of which contained original writings and observations. Yet, he was one of only thousands of African scholars who flourished during Islamic times. The fact is it was under Islam that Africans reached their pinnacle of intellectual development. This was because under its banner all races flourished. Through it Africans, Berbers, Morrocans, Egyptians, Turks, Spaniards, Sicilians, Afghanis, Persians, and Arabs, as well as Europeans, all experienced their grandest social and intellectual achievements.

An excellent contrast is the manner in which slaves were treated in North America. As late as the 1880s it was illegal for African-Americans to pursue learning. The fact is black learning is still under siege. In 1998 in Mississippi the last remaining African-American newspaper facility was fire-bombed. In the Americas racism abounds.

Yet, incredibly, during the height of the slave trade Africans were at the pinnacle of intellectual supremacy. In contrast to the typical perception of African slaves, that is that they were mere savages, education among Africans had reached its highest peak. The slave trade coincided with the era of scholarship at Timbuktu, where tens of thousands of Africans achieved higher education. The fact is thousands, perhaps millions, of these Africans, fully capable of reading and writing, many of them outright scholars, were victims of this catastrophe.

The slave trade was perhaps the most brutal example of human tyranny ever known. Those who perpetrated it were utterly merciless, in fact, diabolical.

No one was immune from the debauchery. The elderly, who were often the most wise or perhaps learned, were treated ruthlessly, since they were of no consequence to the slavers. This debacle was demonstrated by Thomas Bruxton in his book, *The African Slave Trade*. Bruxton describes an original eyewitness account of the brutality of the European slave trade in what is now known as Ethiopia:

"The grown-up men are all killed, and are then mutilated, parts of their bodies being always carried away as trophies; several of the old mothers are killed, while others, frantic with fear and despair, kill themselves. The boys and girls...are then carried off in brutal triumph."

This fully illustrates that the stereotype of African slaves as uncouth primitives is largely fabricated. African Society was built on the family unit, which was, in fact, a highly civilized way of living. What's more, indigenous Africans were highly skillful individuals, who functioned within well established social settings. The fact is during the 16th through the 17th century it was black Africa alone which led the African continent in scholarly achievements. The lighter races of North Africa were at that time in relative intellectual decay. In fact, the European slave trade greatly contributed to the decline in African scholarship. True, some enslaved Africans were primitives. Yet, the majority were talented individuals, especially in the fine crafts. They were also adept at farming. This latter fact was equally a reason for their enslavement as was raw labor. In other words, they were skilled laborers. They also excelled physically, therefore, could endure a massive work load. That is why they were enslaved. The true barbarians, that is the real savages, were not the Africans. Rather, it was those who perpetuated this crime, i.e. the slavers. What's more, it was also those who financed the slavers, that is the wealthy Western elite.

In contrast, Islam, for the first time in history, created the environment of complete racial equality. In fact, regarding Africa it was only under the environment of Islam in which African people produced their greatest scientific achievements. Timbuktu was a consequence of Islamic civilization. Here, tens of thousands of books on the sciences were produced by African scholars. This was because in Islam brutality against other people on the basis of race was unknown. People were assessed for their human potential, not for how they could be manipulated or abused. What's more, the demonization of the races was unknown. The fact is the brutality against the Africans began only after Islamic civilization disintegrated. Thus, Islam acted as a barrier against human monopolization. As a civilization Islam was eliminated in the 15th century.

This is precisely when the African slave trade began.

European, as well as American, civilization was created through the abuse of other peoples. Incredibly, hundreds of millions of people died to create it. In contrast, Islam elevated people to their highest status, who then built civilization. This was a civilization where race, religion, or social status formed no barrier to personal progress. What's more, as mentioned previously according to Briffault during the Islamic Era being a "Muslim" was apparently of no advantage. The only advantage, that is the only distinction, was the extent of an individual's learning. Furthermore, it was not clerical knowledge which was the most greatly admired. Rather, it was exclusively the knowledge of the sciences, that is the practical arts, in which the greatest accolades were earned.

Yet, despite the interest in practical learning a constant moral fabric remained. Islam means submission of the self to the will of God. It was a feature which permeated its civilization. Because of its unique approach, all people were treated equally. The fact is the equal treatment for all was regarded as a means of serving God. In contrast, racism was regarded as a crime. This was why in Islamic institutions the issue of race never arose. In a feat unmatched in history people from all cultures and races attended the Islamic universities, praising the name of God during their studies.

This was, and is, the true Islam. It is the Islam that was so resolutely established by Prophet Muhammad, its original knowledge-seeker. It was this man alone who instructed his followers to traverse the globe in search of knowledge. Incredibly, his dictum emphasized primarily the search for worldly knowledge, that is practical information, which assists the growth and development of humankind.

The European Connection

As demonstrated by the Crusades even in ancient times bigotry against Islam was extensive. It was an era of utter barbarism, which is unmatched in human history. Here, ignorance reigned. Whatever the masses failed to understand, they destroyed. However, after Christians interacted directly with the Muslims their views began to change, albeit slowly. Rather than being feared or hated Islam began to be viewed as the source of a superior civilization, one to be emulated. Ultimately, Europeans began to adopt Islamic customs, including the dress and military code. In fact, Islam was the source for their entire idea of civilization. Yet, unfortunately, they failed to develop an interest in matters of faith. However, materially, they were aware of the Islamic accomplishments and, thus they sought to adopt every possible aspect of it.

According to Western historians the achievements of this divinely inspired science earned the admiration, in fact, awe, of Europeans. They were in awe of it because of what it produced. This implies that it was Islam's material accomplishments more so than its religious tendencies which primarily captivated, as well as motivated, non-Muslims.

Christian Europeans failed to fully comprehend the essence of the Islamic message, that is how it impacts the heart and soul. Yet, even without the penetration of its true spirit, Islam indelibly influenced the West, *materially*. Incredibly, it was only Islam which stimulated the flourishing of Western science, the very science which now denies any role of the creator. In other words, Europe failed to invent science independently. It couldn't be responsible, because, inherently, it was opposed to them. It required a stimulus. The fact is it required a potent source, that is a source which was revolutionary. It had to be revolutionary to such a degree that it could drastically alter established thinking. Islam provided that revolution in thinking. What's more, according to a number of authorities, including the renowned Harvard historian George Sarton, Islam's mighty achievements singlehandedly provoked the Renaissance.

The evidence for the Islamic creation of the Renaissance is vast. For instance, in pre-Renaissance Europe, that is in the 12th through the 14th centuries, there were no scientific books. Scholarly institutions were unknown. Nor were there any public schools. Furthermore, there were no universities. Thus, obviously, without schools there could be no learning. What's more, mandates existed against education. Anyone who sought private learning was held suspect. In fact, Europe became a society of informants. People reported to the ruling class anyone who studied the sciences. As a result, learning could only be attempted under the utmost secrecy. If the lower classes sought to learn the sciences, for instance, slaves, they were tortured and brutally killed. The fact is thousands of individuals were executed simply because they studied the sciences.

Thus, in Middle Age Europe public education was unknown. This lack of education of the masses provided the basis for one of the most diabolical episodes in human history: the Crusades. The ignorant masses regarded people of learning as "enemies of the faith." Incredibly, they regarded the study of the sciences as the work of the devil. Thus, instead of higher learning they reveled in superstition, magic, and pagan rites. This attitude of the European masses explains why the clergy were so successful in provoking warfare. The hate and violence spread by the Crusaders was primarily due to one fact: these warriors were largely illiterate. While they were seemingly Christians in name, intellectually they were barbarians. Yet, barbarism is only grudgingly eradicated, and, thus, it took decades, in fact, centuries, for the Crusaders to incorporate the sophistication of Islam. Ultimately, this occurred, and it was this alone which led to the rapid expansion of Europe.

In the development of Christian Europe Islam provided the universities, where Christians and Jews learned the precise sciences. It also provided the scientific texts, which were, ultimately, translated from the original Arabic. In addition, it provided the libraries. The fact is Islam essentially donated to Europe millions of books, manuscripts, and essays. This alone is compelling evidence of the true source of the revival. According to Thomas Goldstein in his book, *Dawn of Modern*

Science, European scholars came to the lands of Islam to translate its books "in droves." One such scholar spent 50 years in Islamic Spain strictly translating Arabic/Islamic texts. These texts were scoured by hundreds of scholars from all over Europe—England, Spain, Germany, France, Scandinavia, Holland, the Netherlands, and Italy—who translated them into Latin. These texts catapulted book-free, pagan Europe from the depths of intellectual despair to the heights of civilization. Goldstein further claims that the store of knowledge provided by the Muslims was "the most complete" ever produced in history.

Imagine the situation. For nearly ten centuries the development of the sciences in Europe had been completely repressed. Western civilization was seemingly incapable of advancing, and, if Paul Tannery's words are correct, it was in reverse. The Church ordained the torture, death, and/or imprisonment of anyone caught studying the sciences. The preferred "punishment" was burning the victims alive at the stake. Thus, the growth of civilization was completely repressed. Then, suddenly, there was a dramatic change. Europe acquired the intellectual treasures of Islam. The Europeans realized the error of their ways and the deficit, in fact, degradation, that resulted. Thus, they upgraded their existence and based this on the Islamic texts. They adopted the material achievements of Islam and also accepted a significant proportion of its philosophy. The authority of the book, public education, the postal system, paper money, triple coinage, public libraries, educational degrees, the pharmacy, fine architecture, metal inlay, the textile industry, leather crafting, the embroidered cloth, secular modern hospitals, medical specialties, and public hygiene were all established, none of which existed prior to Islam.

Although by name they rarely if ever mentioned the Prophet, Europeans fully subscribed to many of his teachings. Herbal medicine, one of his favorite prescriptions, was thoroughly developed. The value of honey as a medicine became respected. Bathing and personal hygiene were eventually instituted. Public hygiene and sanitation were incorporated. The Prophet's ideas on public education were inculcated. His civilized approach to international diplomacy was practiced. Perfuming the body became popular, as did regular bathing, both of which are his. Doctors began washing their hands and arms up to the elbows, a practice which he originated.

The Renaissance: Its Islamic Roots

The Islamic influence on Europe is indisputable. This is because for Europeans there was no other source of written knowledge. The fact is the concept of public education came exclusively to Europe through Islamic Spain. It was a direct connection, being disseminated from Spain to France and from there to the rest of Europe. The first true European university was in Montpellier, France. Its curriculum and books were exclusively Islamic. As further evidence for this connection Islam maintained a presence in southern France for hundreds of years. Regarding the University of Montpellier recent excavations prove that for its first 100-plus years only Arabic-Islamic books were used. Incredibly, this shows that it took decades, in fact, centuries, before medieval Europeans began developing their own independent science. This was a time when in Europe the concept of the book was unknown. It was a time when independent writing was rare. Rather, people relied exclusively upon the dictates or writings of the clergy. Or, they felt obligated to submit to the authority of ancient scholars, never questioning them. Thus, book learning was an absolute novelty for medieval Europeans so much so that it took hundreds of years before they began publishing their own independent works. Islam provided the basis for such productions. For hundreds of years Europeans merely parroted the Islamic texts. The fact is all the original European universities were based upon the Islamic model, and Islamic books, as well as scholars, were hired to facilitate them. Thus, incredibly, without Islam modern educational institutions would have never developed. This is because only Islam possesses that utterly liberal approach, which is the unbridled service of humankind for the sake of a higher purpose, for the sake of almighty God. Only it places human needs above the desires of the vested few. Were it not for its brave effort to create and disseminate knowledge, Europe would have likely remained in barbarism, perhaps indefinitely.

During the Dark Ages scientific advances in Europe were non-existent. This was because any study of scientific texts was regarded as heresy. In fact, in medieval Europe religious edicts called for the public lynching of all scientists. People lived in fear of being killed or imprisoned simply for pursuing private learning. For instance, Copernicus, who was an amateur astrologer and astronomer, presented his book publically only at his deathbed. What's more, to mix religion with science was regarded as heresy, punishable by what is perhaps the most gruesome of all deaths: being burnt alive. In what was one of the most barbaric episodes in human history thousands of European scholars were imprisoned, tortured, and/or murdered by their own people for the "crime" of attempting to gain knowledge. Thus, in such a hostile environment there was no possibility for science to flourish. The establishment regarded the study of books in fields other than theology as a crime. This policy had a devastating effect upon the potential growth of civilization, fully repressing independent thinking for centuries.

Internally, Europe showed no movement towards an awakening. It was Islam which provided the stimulus. In fact, its influence was so profound that it initiated the Renaissance. This is because the Renaissance was stimulated by reason, that is by relying upon the powers of scientific truths. Thus, it was stimulated by the use of the mind to reject barbaric, archaic, and false beliefs. What's more, incredibly, in what is rarely recognized the entire revolution occurred with minimal if any violence. It was strictly a revolution in thinking. Specific scientific truths neutralized archaic thinking, purging the mind of bias and intolerance. Thus, knowledge alone destroyed barbarism, freeing Europeans from utter darkness. There was a singular source for these truths. Ancient Greece failed to provide them. Instead, as delineated by Goldstein, Briffault, Sarton, Renan, and dozens of other Western historians it was the writings and philosophies of Islam that were the true source. There is no other possibility.

This fact was clearly delineated by J. D. Wallis in his book, *A Treatise of Algebra*. Written in the 1600s it was the first English text on mathematics ever produced. According to Wallis algebra and, in fact, virtually all other European mathematics arose exclusively from one source, and that wasn't the Greeks. Rather, he clearly states that these sciences were exclusively the creations of Islamic (literally, "Arabic") scientists. This finding is utterly crucial. This is because it proves that rather than the Greeks it was the Muslims who modernized, in fact, invented mathematics. The scope of this achievement by Islam is memorialized by the fact that it is modern mathematics which forms the basis of other critical sciences, including astronomy, physiology, physics, geology, chemistry and geography. It was Thomas Goldstein in his book, *Dawn of Modern Science*, who clearly stated that all the modern sciences are Islamic in origin.

Western historians document that during the Dark Ages the data produced by Islam was the only available source for the sciences, including Western sciences. For nearly two centuries, which is approximately the age of the entire existence of the United States, Europe's scholars exclusively read the Arabic/Islamic books. However, despite becoming learned about their content they lacked the sophistication to perform original detailed scientific experiments. They simply relied upon or duplicated the experiments already produced by Islam. The fact is after translating the Islamic books it took European scholars nearly three full centuries before they began conducting their own original scientific experiments. This is an utter testimony to the high degree of scientific advancement achieved by Islam in contrast to the dire level of backwardness in medieval Europe. The point is Islam created the revival, in fact, it originated the sciences, which were then directly adopted by Europe. Prior to Islam Europeans had never developed their own learned civilization. Of note, the ancient Greeks were primarily a Mediterranean people. Thus, because of its systematic approach in the creation of the sciences, Islam originated the very basis of European and, therefore, Western civilization. It did so intellectually, materially, and even architecturally. Yet, incredibly, it was a process which took hundreds of years. Modern civilized peoples, particularly Americans and Europeans, owe Islam immensely. Without it, this modern, sophisticated world would fail to exist.

It was Islam which provided the books for the European awakening. These books contained detailed scientific experiments. Their information was arranged in a methodical fashion. In contrast to the publications of the ancient Greeks, which were largely theoretical, the Islamic ones were highly practical. This is because the purpose of such books was the advancement of human civilization for all peoples, not just the elite. Such experiment-laden and detail-oriented books provided the basis for Europe's scientific revolution. Many of these books, such as Ibn al-Haytham's *Optics*, were filled with highly detailed scientific experiments. Through his sophisticated experimental approach his book alone revolutionized European thinking, directly influencing scholars in all European countries, including England. It was al-Haytham, the author of some 80 books, who singlehandedly introduced Europeans to the science behind vision as well as the entire science of optics and physics. In his books they found detailed scientific experiments. This was Europe's first introduction to scientific experiments. Thousands of such books, rich in scientific efforts, were popularized in Middle Age Europe. The fact is the Islamic books provided European scholars with their first exposure to the most crucial aspect of modern science: the experimental method.

Clearly, the experimental method was unknown to the Greeks, nor was it realized by the Hindus, Byzantines, Babylonians, or Persians. This explains why George Sarton, the premier Harvard historian of science, attributes this method to the scholars of Islam.

Everyone knows that in the sciences learning begins with books. The books can't be based upon mere speculation, that is they must be practical. In other words, they must provide examples of the proper experiments. They must also provide examples of deductive reasoning, that is reasoning based upon non-emotional, practical observations. In the Islamic Empire such books were produced in vast quantities. During this era single libraries contained hundreds of thousands, and in some cases, millions, of books. In contrast, in medieval Europe there were no public libraries or scientific books. Any books which did exist were pre-screened, that is censored, by the Church. Books with scientific content were burned, destroyed, or hidden. While Europe was mired in barbarism, Islamic scholars created millions of books. As European scholars were imprisoned or killed throughout the wide extent of the Islamic Empire hundreds of thousands of scholars studied in absolute freedom. The fact is the "regular" people were also scholars, that is there was no intellectual elite. Even so-called slaves became erudite scholars. What's more, to facilitate scholarly advancement there were thousands of libraries scattered throughout its wide extent. Incredibly, while Islam created and made available tens of millions of books, teaching peoples of all races and faiths scholarly learning, there were virtually no books available in Western Europe. More correctly, there were no books written independently by European scholars. If there were scientific books, they were essentially duplicates of those found in the lands of Islam. This duplication of Islamic books was clearly elucidated by the French historian Renan, who claimed that because of their utter reliance upon Islamic books, prominent early European scholars, such as Roger Bacon and St. Thomas Aquinas, "owed everything" they knew to Islamic scientists. What's more, such statements are supported by recent excavations of early European universities, which utterly prove the Islamic source. There, in certain universities for up to 200 years, which is, incredibly, approximately the time of the existence of the United States, the only source for European learning was Islamic texts.

Without books, learning is nonexistent. The fact is as described in the *Encyclopedia of the History of Arabic Science* the book as we know it today is exclusively an Islamic invention.

This role of Islam in the initiation of the European Renaissance was due to its unique approach. The initial words of the Qur'an commanded the use of the intellect rather than mere reliance on faith. In contrast, the Church relied exclusively on faith, promoting the dictum that "Where reason stops, faith begins." This is a bizarre, in fact, diabolical, concept. The implication is that a religion which refuses to allow the use of reason has something to fear. Would it be, perhaps, that reasoning would uncover false information, and this would ultimately lead to rejection? Could it result in the freedom of thought needed to dispel blind faith?

In medieval Europe any attempt to delve into the sciences, that is to explain the divine presence through the mechanisms of science, was regarded as blasphemous. In fact, such an approach was deemed the work of the devil. Islam took the opposite approach, that is that research and investigation bring the individual closer to God.

With Europe in such a dire state there was no hope for its recovery. Only a massive stimulus could revive it. The stimulus came from a most unexpected source. It was a source free of the dogma, which kept Europe from advancing. It was those initial words of the Qur'an, that is to "Read, and do so in the name of the almighty Lord," which were the original stimuli. It was the Qur'an which demanded that humans rely upon their reason, that is upon the use of their minds, rather than ignorance or old traditions. These words changed the entire world. Essentially, the Qur'an commanded, "Humankind, abandon your former decadent ways and elevate yourself from ignorance to the brilliance of reason. In other words, begin to think for yourself. Remove yourself from the ignorance of mistaken beliefs. Do this by reading, writing, and thinking—by the use of your mind. However, do it in the name of your almighty Lord, the very Lord who originally created you from a mere leech-like clot in a womb. Your origins are truly humble. You were once lowly. You were once obviously completely dependent upon me. Never forget it. Thus, to elevate yourself to the highest level possible, use your intellect. Learn through reading and understanding as much as possible regarding the world about you, that is through using your reason. This is because your Lord is extremely generous, in fact, absolutely gracious in how He blesses you, and the ability to use the mind is perhaps His greatest blessing. Do not take for granted that what you knew previously is all that is necessary. Your knowledge is limited, and there is much to learn. What's more, He alone has taught you learning through the written word, that is the ability to write. In fact, this is how I, your Lord, teach human beings what they were unaware of.' The message continues with, essentially, 'Once you have gained this knowledge, you are responsible to behave decently. Thus, after you were in such need of Us and were so utterly dependent upon Us do not make yourself aloof from Us, that is after you have become secure. What's more, do not use the abilities We have granted you to spread corruption and harm amongst My creation. If you do so, you are denying My truths. Are you unaware that I am fully aware of your actions? If you persist in committing wrongful acts, your fate will be sealed. I will inflict upon you My punishment, and when that happens, there will be no one to help you.' Plus, as is found elsewhere in the Qur'an, conceptually, 'after you have gained the knowledge with which I have blessed you, guard yourself from becoming arrogant, deceitful, and self-righteous, because such behavior would be a crime worse than living in ignorance.'

Thus, the Muslims regarded these commands seriously. Stimulated to work hard as a divine duty, they sought to advance the cause of civilization and science at any expense. They worked exceedingly hard to create positive results. Knowledge was accumulated in the name of God rather than for self-advancement or personal gain. The Muslims became internationally renowned, yet remained humble. During the Islamic Era the arrogance so typical of intellectuals today was unknown. Pride of discovery, that is desiring all credit for the self, was frowned upon. In fact, in scholarly circles arrogance was regarded as an aberrant behavior.

Because of their unique approach to learning, the scholars of Islam universally shared their discoveries. Thus, in contrast to the attitude of the European scientists of the 17th through 19th century there was no attempt to hoard or protect discoveries for personal gain. Rather than assuming the credit for themselves, God was given the credit. Thus, prominent Islamic scholars had little or no interest in making themselves the "authorities." Rather, their goal was gaining knowledge for the service of God, for the sake of pleasing Him, and for the purpose of aiding humanity. Thus, they initiated scientific study with a motive far different than those of today: the service of God versus the service of the self.

The Islamic approach is far more sophisticated than that of today's scientists. This is because today scientists often seek personal gain at the expense of others—at the expense of this very earth. In contrast, with Muslim scientists, that is the original scientists of the Islamic Empire, the goal was to improve the human condition. In their view this was the most elegant way to serve God. For instance, under Islam genetic engineering, that is the uncontrolled altering of the genetic code for purposes of corporate profits, would be banned. This is because the benefit is vastly outweighed by the harm. It would also be banned because evidence is lacking proving safety. Until firm evidence could be offered to prove absolute safety, both for humans and the remainder of this planet, it would be prohibited. Islam propounds other more well known prohibitions. However, all the prohibitions are for the benefit of humanity. Currently, thorough evidence exists that the unnatural alteration of the genetic code through genetic engineering is damaging this planet as well as animals and humans. Bizarre rashes, severe allergic reactions, asthma attacks, muscle wasting diseases, and even sudden death are associated with the intake of genetically altered foods. The fact is there is no assurance that such foods are safe. On the contrary the indication is that they are toxic. The fact is, surely, their regular intake will lead to the destruction of living beings and, ultimately, the destruction of civilization. Once the genetic systems are thoroughly corrupted every conceivable decimation will occur, both to the environment and living beings. Vast unheard of diseases will strike. Deaths, perhaps by the millions, will occur. Thus, this is the key difference between an Islamic civilization and the typical Western type: under Islam genetically engineered foods would be deemed unproven and potentially hazardous. Thus, their production would be prohibited.

Genetically engineered foods and seeds have already caused irreparable damage to this planet. What's more, genetically engineered foods, which are prolific in the American food supply, are a major cause of human disease. Bizarre illnesses, such as unusual rashes and respiratory disorders, are directly connected. What's more, an epidemic of sudden deaths among grade-schoolers, as well as teenagers, has been tied to the intake of these foods. Genetically engineered foods or food additives are common in school food programs as well as fast food. The fact is American children, as well as teenagers and college students, are dying directly as a result of the intake of these foods. Yet, sadly, this devastation of the food supply was utterly avoidable. The "patenting" of the food supply is diabolical, since the issue of safety is never addressed. Rather, corporate profits are solely the issue. Because of its unique and direct approach to what is lawful and prohibited, Islam would have prevented such a calamity. This may be one reason it is under siege. Its laws directly conflict with corporate greed.

Regarding learning, Islam created a novel concept: the unrestricted sharing of data. It preaches love for humanity and practices it by sharing its achievements, even with its enemies. Islam's method is to give independently of worldly gain. In other words, it is to give exclusively for the sake of almighty God. Thus, for the first time in history intellectual interchange was promoted without restriction.

Islam performed another original feat. It offered its learning to all other civilizations. Ultimately, it did so even to its detriment. Its commitment to humanity was so great that if the dissemination of learning was to even compromise its existence, so be it.

In ancient civilizations such an approach was unknown. Learning was held in strict control by the ruling elite. In contrast, Islam shared all of its learning, even its weapons technology. Incredibly, according to thorough research by Reinuad and Favé it was the Muslims who, ultimately, during the 12th century provided the formula for gunpowder to the Europeans.

This unbridled sharing of knowledge dramatically altered the course of civilization. The fact is as is documented by Thomas Goldstein in his book, *Dawn of Modern Science*, today's advanced, education-driven world is strictly an Islamic production. This is true because no society prior to it shared its knowledge bank. Thus, when all previous ancient civilizations collapsed, so did their knowledge. This was certainly true of ancient Babylon, Egypt, and Greece. Their knowledge store was only recovered centuries later, that is what remained of it. This greatly stalled the development of civilization. Islam drastically altered this cycle. Its knowledge was directly absorbed by Europe. This is because it was the only civilization which upheld the love of humanity as its primary goal. The fact is its major objective is to fuel the positive growth of humanity. Previously, the civilizations of the world kept their scientific and medical learning in the hands of the upper class. Thus, public education was unknown. By creating the first system of public education it was Islam which dismantled these barriers. The fact is for anyone living under its auspices pursuing an education was deemed a divinely-ordained duty.

When Islam arrived, the world had sunk to its lowest condition. Crime and social defilement were the norm. In Europe myths, magic, and superstition reigned. Education of the masses was unheard of and scientific investigation was nonexistent. Incredibly, while medieval Europe was entrenched in religious dogma, regarding material accomplishments and scientific learning as the works of the devil, the Muslim world built the most elegant, refined, and decorative, that is the most materialistically-rich and sophisticated civilization ever known.

Yet, more importantly, the books, which stimulated the birth of the West, were strictly Islamic. True, there were books in Europe. However, these were exclusively in the possession of the clergy and elite. The public had no access to scientific or historical texts. Nor if they did could they understand them. Thus, as originally described by S. H. Pasha the concept of the school, university, and library—the concept of public education—all arose from Islam. What's more, it was also the source of the actual books, that is the easy-to-understand textbooks. In contrast, the Greek works were impractical. In other words, they were user unfriendly. This is because they were based upon theories rather than practical experiments.

In Islam there is no ruling elite. There is no attempt to disguise knowledge from the public. The fact is the latter is regarded as a crime. Thus, in a truly Islamic system the rulers, while in a position of utter power and respect, are the servants of the people. There is no other system which offers this method.

Motivated by Prophet Muhammad the Muslims, as well as their Christian and Jewish associates, gathered the global literature and converted it for public use. Thus, singlehandedly, Islam revived, in fact, popularized, the written word, which, since the time of ancient Greece, had become virtually extinct. Plus, it created learning in a form that could readily be utilized: by everyone, even people of different languages. This is the invaluable and permanent contribution of Islam to civilization.

The Definition of Islam

The practices and/or beliefs of many religions have been observed, presented, and discussed. In the Western world certain aspects regarding the nature of Christianity, Judaism, and possibly Hinduism and Buddhism are understood. However, comparatively little is known about Islam. Once regarded as a local religion meant for Arabs or Middle Easterners now it is known that Islam is global. Yet, few if any Westerners understand what it means.

Islam is an Arabic word, which means peace. It is a peace between all creatures and their creator. It is the peaceful submission to the will and rule of God.

In Islam this creator is the God of all things, the absolute Master of the universe. He isn't a select God belonging to a particular religion, race, or tribe. Islam proposes that God is one, His guidance is one, His creation is one, and His highest creation, humankind, is one.

While it is described as a religion, ideally, Islam is meant as a way of life. That is why it is named after its meaning rather than a specific group or individual. Here, God is different than the concept popular today. This is no distant God, disconnected and unavailable. Rather, as originally described by S. H. Pasha the Islamic view, that is the Qur'anic view, is that He is intimately involved with this world. As a creator He fashions the molds for designing all that exists. As a re-creator He constantly designates which corrective changes need to be made for the universe's proper evolution. In fact, His powers within this universe are unlimited. He alone decides what He will create and simply does it. That is the Islamic view of almighty God.

Compared to other religions, Islam is unique. This is because all other major religions derive their names from a certain people, place, or tribe. Christianity, which is named after Jesus Christ, and Judaism, which is named after the tribe of Judea, are examples. In contrast, Islam is named after its meaning. The Arabic root means both peace and submission. Therefore, a person who follows Islam is literally "one who submits." Thus, by submitting to God the individual achieves the ultimate peace, both in this existence as well as in the future one.

The Qur'an accents this tone, that is it disassociates itself from any specific people, time, or place. It further claims that religion is a matter of definition rather than a mere "group" to associate with. Thus, in this view the religion of God is represented simply by being of 'Islam' heart and soul. It is to submit willingly to the will, rule, and way of life of almighty God. It proposes that for a human being to ultimately succeed it is necessary to follow God's way. In contrast, the human way ultimately leads to failure. What's more, no one has any preference in this submission. Anyone can accept it at any time or place. Thus, from the Islamic point of view all people are equal, because all are required to submit. This may explain why Islam is the most universal of all religions.

Even so, Islam was never meant to develop into a religion to simply follow. The mere adherence to ritual alone or a club-like or social belonging was never its goal. In fact, this is its antithesis. If it has become so, it is the result of human influence. This is because Islam represents a way of life. It is the means to revive hearts as well as minds. Thus, its purpose is to be a force for change. Its objective is to alter the course of history by altering the beliefs, the behaviors, and, particularly, the thinking, of human beings. Without change it is useless.

Law and Order—an Islamic Concept

Science has confirmed that there is an intelligible order in the universe, an order based upon laws. Yet, who is enacting and enforcing the universal legislation?

The constitution of the United States originated as a code of laws, which have been instituted by this nation's leaders for over 200 years. Constitutional leaders are not limited to presidents. There is also the Supreme Court, as well as local leaders, like governors and mayors. Even the proper operation of the local "club" is dependent on the rule of its potentate. The point is every system requires a leader. For example, in order to operate effectively the United States is dependent upon leaders and legislators. Thus, would the vast universe that surrounds us be an exception? Wouldn't it also be dependent upon deliberate leadership? What's more, is it plausible that there are several leaders for the universe, as there are for this world, each with his own powers of jurisdiction? Or, is there only One, a single Commander-in-Chief, who administrates all?

For a moment turn your head to the sky: do you see or sense the universal organization? Look again; do you sense that Force, that incredibly pervasive and inconceivable Power? Do you see that it has order and that it is free from fault? Do you sense anything besides absolute organization? In other words, do you see any evidence of chaos? What's more, does it appear as anything other than one universe, rather than multiple or conflicting systems? Thus, again, does it make sense that there are several rulers, that is multiple divine powers, each likely to compete with each other? Regarding this concept of "the gods": does this make sense, or, is there One Who rules all?

Americans, as well as Europeans, follow the rule of law. Yet, someone has to make those laws. Furthermore, the laws must be enforced, otherwise, mayhem, in fact, tyranny, will reign. Who, then, makes the laws that govern the vast universe? What's more, who enforces them? Common sense would indicate that there is one Power alone, almighty God, Who is the supreme lawmaker, as well as lawgiver, Who is the President of presidents and the Ruler of rulers. Islam places the role of God in this world in perspective by saying no president, king, or dictator could rule if it wasn't for Him Who built lands to be governed, Who gave men the potential to lead, men who even when rejecting the position of God must ultimately follow Him. Why must they do so? This is because the very cells and organs of their bodies, in fact, their very atoms and molecules, would cease to operate without adhering to His universal rules. It is easier to simply adhere to His rule. This is far easier and more productive than resisting it. Plus, if a Being of this magnitude provides humankind with rules, why follow anything else? People follow the rule of their mighty governments. Islam claims that God almighty is the true Governor, who must be followed.

It is a fact that atoms follow rules. All biological beings also adhere to them. Thus, there must be a rule-maker. Humans are unable to make the rules. Who else could make them besides almighty God? What's more, Who's rule should be followed, God's or mortal man's? The point is humans fear the consequences of defying social authority such as the police or federal government. Islam says that if there must be fear it should be of the ultimate authority, the One who truly controls all: God almighty Himself.

Science states that the atom is an organized system. It consists of a nucleus encircled by layers of orbiting electrons. Its exact nature is a matter of speculation. While no one has ever seen the atom, the Islamic view is that its Creator sees it. What's more, in His infinite wisdom He designed it as the basic building block of all that exists. In fact, the Qur'an uses the term "atom-weight" conceptually in various parables. The atom itself is supremely organized. What's more, the Islamic view is that all that exists is highly organized, because God Himself is a systematic being. What is the atom other than a miniature model of our own solar system? Can't the earth and other planets be viewed as "electrons" in their various subshells orbiting a solar nucleus? Here again is evidence for a designing Power, whose systematic blueprint permeates all levels of existence. The fact is it is the Lord of the universe alone Who can establish such relative perfection on all scales. In contrast, could accidental evolution cause such a fantastic, repetitive design? This is certainly unlikely. In fact, if the rules of science are used as a determinant, that is the rules which humans live by, accidental creation would appear impossible.

Only humans violate the rule of law. Certainly, nonhumans never violate it. For instance, other mammals, such as pets—cats, dogs, canaries, etc.—are naturally predictable. They never deviate from their established behaviors. Because of their ability to use higher thought, humans may choose to deviate from their natural instincts. Yet, this violation occurs only in the mind or spirit, never in the body. This is because the human body is obligated to follow specific laws. Thus, it must submit to its natural tendencies. An excellent example is the living cell. It consistently follows specific rules, never deviating from them. While little is known about its exact functions, what is known is that it is highly organized and perfectly designed. According to *Scientific American*'s *The Living Cell* the cells of the human body operate with such a high degree of complexity that they perform feats which are beyond comprehension. In other words, the cells perform functions which humans will never be able to understand. The structure of such cells is described as "highly organized" as well as "fine." The cellular components are regarded as "complicated systems." The use by the *Scientific American* of the term "systems" connotes a high degree of organization. It is a degree of organization that is so perfect and so utterly complex that human beings could never duplicate it, regardless of the time, technology, or effort. Chance evolution could never result in such a system. Thus, it must be a divine creation.

Human beings benefit enormously from the universe's law and order. Every aspect of its refined structure appears to be geared for human benefit. For instance, there is no concern that the earth will suddenly leap from its orbit to float aimlessly into space. Nor is there the worry that the atoms in our bodies will lose their integrated form to leave us in a lifeless heap. Rather, the systems are maintained in their unalterable state by a power beyond us. It is a power over which humans have no influence. What's more, it is the only power that could conceivably alter these forms. In other words, it is the only force which could create the bizarre or miraculous. Yet, this Power appears to follow a more scientific and/or predictable approach to the operations of this world. Bizarre and miraculous events, in other words, events which defy the laws of nature, are utterly rare. Instead, apparently, God causes the system to follow its own pathway. He intercedes only under the most unusual circumstances. Thus, even for God the rules are rarely violated. Instead of miracles that defy universal laws all that exists follows a deliberate and predictable plan. In other words, humans can predict the events and/or consequences. Incredibly, the way this universe operates never violates the laws of science. This is why Islam claims that objects of this world are not governed by evolution or mere chance but are, rather, guided in perfection by the Supreme Governor, Who is the creator of the universal laws which the atom, the earth, the solar system, the universe, and the human body itself must obey.

Yet, this issue of obedience to God is the very basis of Islam. Here, the existence of a single all-powerful God is never questioned. According to it He alone made human beings. He provided them with all that they require. He gave them the ability to see, hear, and think. He provided them with every type of support, from lovely companions to food, pleasure, and drink. Therefore, humans should completely obey Him. They should only worship Him. No other power is worthy of submission.

The tendency is that most people obey their parents. The respect for parents can be extreme. People often submit obediently, even if the parents are in the wrong. Thus, usually, people feel obligated to honor whatever parents request. Children and adolescents may even fear the consequences of disobedience. Even for adults there is the desire to obey them. Yet, in this universe there is a far greater authority, who, reasonably, is to be respected as we might respect our parents, rather incredibly more so. This authority is the supreme and almighty God, the great caretaker, the ultimate parent. We love our parents. Could we learn to love God?

The idea of fearing God is alien to most people. Thus, many individuals resist it. Yet, incredibly, people submit to extreme fears about human authorities, including parents, authority figures, and/or government agencies. At a minimum He should be feared like a child fears his mother or father. Yet, unlike a parent, who could err in judgement, almighty God's assessments are always correct. In other words, He is the most just of all authorities. He always assesses humans accurately and fairly. Thus, to obey Him, even to fear Him, is the highest of all achievements. This is because to do so is to develop the most elegant of all relationships with Him. It is to place Him and the self in their proper position. It is to hold God as the true source of power. It is to determine the ultimate purpose of a person's life, that is to above all serve Him. Compared to our earthly parents God is unique. He never demands respect for His own gain. Rather, He commands that humans fear Him alone, strictly for their own benefit. This is so that they can prepare for the inevitable meeting with Him in the afterlife.

It is common for individuals to love fellow humans: a spouse, friend, child, or parent. However, to love God is to achieve it to an even higher degree. To hold God as the ultimate parent is to regard Him as loving and compassionate, never as stern. It is not to burden the self with excessive regulations. The demands upon us by such a being are rather limited. Rather, He allows humans a wide breadth in what they may do. If a parent is true, he loves his offspring. If a child is true, he loves his parents. God loves us, and to reciprocate humans must love, as well as respect, Him. This is because He is the ultimate source: the parent of all. This is the decision all humans must make, that is to be with God—their true parent—or to be without him. It is each person's decision. Yet, to choose Him accomplishes a monumental objective: to gain the greatest success, both in this life and the next.

Chapter Five

The Qur'an and Modern Science

The Qur'an seeks to educate people, specifically about the immense blessings provided by God. This is so that people can feel a sense of love and gratitude for God and His creation. This issue, that is gratitude for His blessings, is the focal point of its message. God is described as creating the heavenly bodies, and, particularly, this earth, for humanity's benefit. In this regard He instructs people to be grateful, that is for their own sake. The existence of the sun as a provider of warmth and light, the moon as a satellite and a source of reflective light, and the alternation of night and day, one providing an opportunity for rest and the other for work and pleasures, and also the wholesome and nutritious foods on this earth: all are described as blessings, specifically created for the benefit of humankind.

Islam also claims that when He created humans God had a special situation in mind. Here, the human being is distinguished from other creatures. This is because only humans are granted the powers of reasoning. Humans are also unique, because they have free choice in distinguishing right from wrong, helpful from harmful, and good from evil. The Qur'an claims that the creation of human beings is for a specific purpose: to serve as God's representatives on earth. Therefore, there is a purpose for life, all based upon laws created by Him.

Islam holds that God truly loves humankind. This is why He sent revelation. It is why He sent laws. It is also why He sent instructors, that is prophets, to show the correct way. Giving of their love, the prophets are specifically sent to help humankind.

With this system God adheres to certain laws. Islam holds that He knows best how to communicate with humans. This is because He designed the human brain as well as its most volatile attribute: human emotions, and thus, He realizes how weak humans truly are. In other words, He understands the consequences of failing to guide such free-willed, vulnerable beings. In contrast to animals, which strictly follow instincts, humans have the ability to choose their destinies. Therefore, from the Islamic viewpoint humans can either select the right or wrong course. Here, God decided to use a means of communication to present humans with guidance regarding how they should behave. Surely, God the creator would use a sensible means to communicate with His creatures. For instance, to best communicate with a monkey another monkey is ideal. Similarly, the best means to communicate with a human is another human, not a god or angel. In other words, people respond most readily to what is familiar. This explains the science behind the system of prophethood.

Again, why must God communicate to humans? Since human beings are incapable of physically perceiving a divine power, God must provide a means of communication, which they can perceive. This is because of their free-willed nature. They can either choose to worship God or reject Him. They can either spread goodness and kindness, or they can spread corruption, destruction, and devastation.

Muslims, Christians, and Jews believe that God communicated His laws, rules, and regulations for living, through the means of prophethood. Rules are needed in all aspects of this universe. According to Islam humankind is no exception.

Islam holds that the prophet is a special human, because he is inspired and guided directly by God. Thus, he is given revelation from the divine source. All prophets, Abraham, Moses, Jesus, and Muhammad, along with countless others, are equal in the sense that they presented the same message from the same God. Muslims believe that when humanity degenerates, the arrival of the prophet, bearing divinely inspired instructions, helps uplift it. Therefore, when the prophet dies and his divine instructions are diluted or altered, lost in the mysteries of history, then human society, lacking in the freshness and mercy of divine guidance, decays. In fact, without the guidance from prophethood utter corruption reigns. When the God-loving and -fearing people of an age are exhausted, killed, or die off, and no sense of God's instructions remain, then according to Islam the purpose behind life itself is lost.

In this life things often abruptly come to an end. In the planetary and animal world the majority of even the most efficiently adapted species eventually becomes extinct. The fact is over the eons millions of species suffered extinction. The human being lives on the average a little more than seventy years. Ultimately, regarding this earth each individual suffers his own sense of extinction. In the case of prophethood Muslims also believe that this had its extinction, that God would choose a certain man in a certain society, just as He chose other men in other societies. The distinguishing factor is that this certain man would be the end of a continuum, the seal of all prophethood. He would be a man sent for everyone to know. This is the position held by the Prophet Muhammad in Islam.

What is the implication of the end of prophethood? It is that since humankind had lost and diluted the teachings and divine books of other pious men, the last instructor must bring instructions, which are undiluted and incorruptible. It means that he must bring instructions that represent a complete code for all time to come. This is so that these instructions can reach the people of future generations, who lack a divine messenger to guide them. It is illogical that there would be several messengers and, therefore, several codes. This would lead to utter confusion, in fact, mayhem. Only one code is necessary.

This is far from a statement against a direct role with people for almighty God. He may readily inspire whomever He desires. Even after Muhammad people will be inspired. In fact, He is constantly inspiring them. It merely means that there will be *no other divine book directly revealed to a prophet.* It also means that Muhammad is the last and universal messenger of God. In other words, there will be no other divinely-ordained prophets whose words and practices must be followed. In other words, the book which he bore is the last opportunity to procure a divine text. Nor will there be any other prophets whose rules and regulations can be deemed true. Nor will there be any other who will teach an exact and accurate system for living. In other words, after the Qur'an there will be no other manuscript which can be directly and exclusively attributed to God. This statement may be readily tested. Simply attempt to find another book of guidance that is free of error. To do so carefully scrutinize any such document in print. There is no other such book.

Most people value their lives. Regarding critical issues people wouldn't knowingly entrust their lives to someone who could be inadequate, perhaps incompetent. For instance, for most people there would be great hesitation to undergo a procedure by a surgeon who is obviously incompetent or to ride as a passenger with a known dangerous driver. If self protection is so important in this existence, what about the preparations for the afterlife? Wouldn't it make sense to entrust those preparations to the One who is fully competent, the Being Who knows all? What's more, if God specifically sent a messenger with guidance and if such a messenger were rejected, who else is there to follow?

Muslims believe that the Qur'an is the book which contains this guidance. They regard it as a complete source of divine instruction, revealed to the unlettered Muhammad. They deem it as an undiluted text, free of human interpolations. Similarly, such a divine source, the Torah, was given to Moses, and the Gospel, to Jesus. Regarding the latter evidence exists of human influence. Because of this, Muslims believe God revealed the Qur'an as the final text. Plus, they believe it has been divinely protected. This was why it was carefully written down, as well as memorized, as it was revealed. What's more, it was not revealed exclusively for the Prophet Muhammad and/or his followers. They were merely the medium. It was sent for all humankind.

Again, Muslims believe that the Prophet Muhammad received the last divine text. However, the fact that he received it is no reason to give him any special position. He was merely a prophet like the rest of God's chosen. In fact, the Qur'anic description, that is that he is "merely a prophet like the previous ones" clearly implies his universal, non-racial role. Thus, the Qur'an emphasizes that he is only a human being. His only distinction was that he was chosen to bear God's final message. The Prophet himself fretted that his followers might hold him excessively in awe, to the point of adoration. In fact, he warned them against such behavior. Yet, many of his followers, in their ignorance, venerate him, for instance, at his supposed tomb in Medina. True, Medina is a religious site of the highest significance, but not because of a corpse. Incredibly, despite the fact that he died long ago many of his followers even hope for his approval or aid. This is a type of paganism, practiced by millions of individuals. Yet, the Prophet himself made it clear that, ultimately, he can aid no one. The fact is this man stated categorically that there is only one source of aid: God almighty Himself.

Obviously, from the tone of the Qur'an this man was sent as an agent for the entire human race. Anyone who regards him as a prophet for a specific group or race has utterly violated his way. Thus, the distinction is simply the fact that of all the messages in existence the revelation he bore is the most recent, current, and accurate. In other words, it is free from human-derived corruptions. The fact is regardless of anyone's beliefs in respect to such a revelation evidence is lacking that it originated from a human source. What's more, history illustrates that the Qur'an is a corruption-free text, that is humans have failed to alter it. Nor has it been reconstructed over the centuries. Thus, it is the means for 21st century humans to gain direct access to God. Add to this the ways of the prophet and there arises a complete system for understanding the methods of almighty God.

The prophet of Islam was completely different than the typical leaders of today. This is because he was a man of the general public. He loved them, and they loved him. They loved him because of who he was, more so than what he preached.

His behavior, that is his unbridled love for humanity, was the only reason he was successful. Had he relegated himself to pomp and self-glory, that is to special privilege, he would have assuredly failed. Nor did he claim divinity or special status, that is he never elevated himself above others. Rather, while he was of a distinguished personality he was essentially one of the regular people. What's more, since Islam offers no support for sainthood, prophets are regarded as human beings like all others. Thus, the Prophet lived and thrived directly among the people. He also died among them, that is he was merely human.

This man bore no halo. Nor did he wear a special robe. In every respect he was the peoples' friend. In contrast to other world leaders, who distance themselves from the populace, he was consistently engaged in daily events. The fact is he was always accessible. He gave freely of his love and was also thoroughly loved. He dedicated himself to the people, and they also dedicated themselves to him. He served them resolutely but also accepted service. He gave all manner of gifts and also graciously received them. He thrilled in the zest of life, but also endured pain and sadness. He laughed and also cried deeply. The fact is he lived much as people today live. Yet, he brought to humanity something utterly profound: the sublime and mighty authority of heart-nourishing revelation. In fact, the main difference between Prophet Muhammad and the previous prophets is simply the Qur'an itself.

The Message and Purpose of the Qur'an

The Qur'an is a more vast revelation than the previous ones. It is also more comprehensive. If a high quality translation can be procured, it is generally easier to understand than the Bible and contains fewer in-depth stories. However, this is not a critique of the Bible, as it also has its value. Yet, the point is the Qur'an is far more than a history or storybook, although it does contain brief exposés regarding prophethood. What's more, in its delivery no race or religion is given preference. Rather, it addresses humanity in general.

The Qur'an delivers its message directly to the individual. The fact is it speaks precisely to a person's heart. Its interest is human beings, and its focus is human souls.

The Qur'an frequently mentions the prophets. This is in order to provide lessons for human benefit. Muhammad is referred to only rarely and with no greater frequency than many other prophets. For instance, in section three the Qur'an depicts the preaching of Christ, saying, in essence, "My people, the fact is the God I worship is the Lord of all. So, to remain on the right path serve Him alone." Mary is described in considerable detail, being the only woman mentioned by name. Abraham and Moses are given extensive representation, more so than Muhammad. The fact is the emphasis on Moses is considerably greater than on the former. This is evidence of almighty God's wisdom. He knows that people resist whatever is new, especially in regard to matters of faith. He realizes that people remain in what they regard as comfort zones, rarely changing from what they regard as familiar. He knows that peoples' pride interferes with any rational thinking, causing them to hold fiercely to established ways. He understands that people only rarely have open minds. Thus, he emphasizes a source of common understanding, that is the story of Moses and his followers. This is because all monotheistic religions agree that Moses was a true prophet. Therefore, obviously, God does all that is possible to guide humans. He makes every attempt to find common ground. He gives little room for a position such as, "I can't believe in your way, because it is different than mine." From the Qur'anic point of view far be it an issue of one book versus another, one religion in contrast to another, one way of life over another: it is merely God's way or the way of disbelief. Yet, despite clear evidence of the truth the question is are people willing to respond?

In addition to the recognition of God as the creator, the angels, and all the various true prophets of old, the Qur'an demands of its readers a rather profound purpose, something never before clearly elucidated: human advancement. The fact is a thorough review of its contents reveals that its primary purpose is to create a certain environment, that is the environment of 'Islam.' It is an environment that results from placing God as the ruler versus mortal men. Ultimately, it is the environment of sophistication, elegance, and tolerance within all civilization. There is another reason the Qur'an is different from previous scriptures. This is because it was carefully preserved. From the beginning of his mission the Prophet understood the importance of the written word. He knew from the first revelation, that is, essentially, "Read in your Lord's name, the One who creates, who creates humans originally from a low-level organism, that clot-like thing which clings...who taught humankind the ability to write...," that it was his responsibility to record it. The "Read" concept was the only one he was given for a period of three years. This caused him to take its meaning seriously. Thus, he understood that only through the advancement of the intellect would God's system succeed. What's more, because of this divine emphasis upon the importance of knowledge, he was always accompanied by scribes, who captured the revelation as it occurred. Nothing was left to mere memory. All was recorded.

While it is realized that belief in it is a matter of personal choice, the fact is in terms of content the Qur'an is irrefutable. This is because it is free of human influence. In other words, since it was written by a non-human source it is devoid of the inevitable errors in human thinking. Its method of revelation is also impossible to deny. This is because it was revealed to a man who was illiterate. What's more, this man had no prior interest in book learning. He never previously wrote a single word. He never before lectured or preached. In fact, prior to the revelation he kept primarily to himself. He was a quiet, private person, and he showed no interest in politics or public recognition. What's more, he was disinterested in the accumulation of wealth and riches, whether before his prophethood or afterwards, when vast riches were in his control.

This man regarded the teaching of the Qur'an as a moral duty. He taught it strictly for the pleasure of God. He promoted it exclusively for the advancement of humanity. Regarding personal motives history proves he had none. On the contrary, in terms of world leaders it was this man alone, who gave of himself, materially, emotionally, and spiritually, to the general population. What's more, he did so even to his own detriment.

Another unique aspect is how well the Qur'an relates to modern times. Despite the fact that it is a seventh century document its statements, as well as origin, completely coincide with modern scientific findings. Regarding the sciences it describes material details, as well as discoveries, that defy a human source. Some of these, for instance, the statement that there exist numerous earth-like worlds, still remain undiscovered. The fact is a careful investigation of its contents reveals that it contains scientific facts unknown at its time as well as certain facts which have only recently been confirmed.

Thus, regardless of anyone's specific beliefs only one conclusion is plausible: this was not written by any mortal man.

The Science of the Qur'an

The Qur'an isn't meant as a book of science. Rather, it is a moral guide. However, certain aspects of it are clearly scientific. A primary scientific aspect relates to its preservation. This is because today's Qur'an represents the original material revealed to Prophet Muhammad, that is it has never been altered. Nor have its contents been diluted or fragmented. As described by S. H. Pasha the point is whatever else this book might be it is precisely, to the letter, the same as presented by the Prophet Muhammad some 1400 years ago. It hasn't been edited or revised. Nor has it been fragmented into numerous doctrines. The fact is in terms of its content, as well as its value to humankind, the Qur'an is the only book which has remained precisely the same despite the passage of over 1400 years.

Some may dispute the issue of the Qur'an's validity. Others may claim it is a human fabrication. Yet, these views are readily dispelled. This is because if it were man-made, numerous contradictions would be found in it. This is true especially as it relates to the sciences. Regardless of who wrote it a seventh century document would be devoid of accurate scientific and astronomical facts. During that era scientific inquiry was unknown.

Furthermore, in terms of its overall message if it were a man-made document, it would lack continuity. Arising in such an illiterate, barbaric society it would be a mere jumble of ideas, which would be incomprehensible. Rather than concepts beneficial to the human being the lusts of the self would be promoted. Nothing productive could be expected. Plus, its contents would be readily proven false. What's more, it would be impossible to gain personal guidance from it, that is guidance on sudden demand, a characteristic exclusively Qur'anic.

True, the Qur'an contains a wide range of information. Thus, some of it may fail to immediately apply to daily circumstances. However, there is great value even in such details. This is because the Qur'an provides regulations helpful for the advancement of civilization. These details, or rules, are of value to prevent people from tyrannizing each other. Yet, the Qur'an is characterized primarily by a single theme: the recognition of the mighty creative powers of God, the comparatively limited power of humans, that is their dependence upon Him, the responsibility of human beings to worship Him, the human *need* to be grateful to Him, the responsibility to do good to the fellow man, the importance of common decency, and the ultimate resurrection and return to Him.

The Qur'an is regarded exclusively as a divine text. This issue is never questioned by its adherents. Adversaries may question it. Yet, can they offer any historical or scientific evidence to dispute it?

It is realized that the concept that it is exclusively from God is a matter of belief. No one can be forced to believe it. However, common sense can help determine if it is truly from God. For instance, in the seventh century A.D. could anyone have known of its concepts? Rather, could any team of men have known them? This is readily determined by simply reading it. While it is true that the individual may choose not to believe in its divine origin, even so, its contents provide irrefutable proof that it is from God. Yet, this is far from an attempt to prove the superiority of one religious book over another, one group above another. Rather, it is merely to delineate the actual status of the Qur'an, that is as an extraterrestrial text written and delivered for the sake of humankind. Thus, from the Qur'an's own point of view it was never meant as a book for a single man and his followers. They were just the medium for receiving it, that is for absorbing it, in an original, ancient language. Its aim is infinitely greater: humankind as a whole. What's more, its objective is regeneration, that is of human souls.

The claim that the Qur'an was written by Prophet Muhammad is readily dispelled. This is because its contents fully indicate an extraterrestrial origin. Plus, whatever it contains thoroughly withstands scientific scrutiny. The Qur'an contains scientific facts. The question is, how did these facts arise? This man, while insightful, was no scientist. His inability to read and write is well known. To advance the sciences reading and writing is a requirement. Muhammad could accomplish neither. Yet, incredibly, billions of people apparently believe that this man wrote the Qur'an.

The idea that he wrote the Qur'an is implausible. Modern scientific facts alone dispute this. This is because this book matches precisely modern findings in astronomy, physics, chemistry, biology, and medicine. For instance, this man could have never known how an embryo forms from beginning to end, which is described fully and precisely in the Qur'an. The latter, i.e. the system of embryology, is a finding only of the latest science. Who else would know this other than God? Could a seventh century man of no formal learning know that the heavenly bodies spin in their orbits and float in space? Could such a man know as stated in the Qur'an that the earth is spherical, rather, oblong? Could he have known, this man of the barren desert, who never so much as saw an ocean or forest, that all life on earth developed originally in a watery mineral-rich soup? Would he have understood that the majority of the weight of the human body is water? These are 20th century discoveries. It would be impossible for them to be discovered in antiquity. The ancients speculated about human origins, however, their theories were erroneous. What's more, there are no theories in the Qur'an: only scientific facts. Such facts could only be determined through intensive research. Muhammad was an illiterate desert dweller. He conducted no scientific research.

There is another reason that Muhammad couldn't have written this book. The Qur'an was revealed segmentally in a systematic fashion. People who write books labor over their manuscripts until they are completed. They review them repeatedly, constantly editing the manuscript into final form. The Qur'an underwent no alterations. It was simply revealed. What's more, rather than being presented as a single book it was revealed as segments, in some cases short bursts, which were sent to directly deal with certain events. In this regard it was written down as it was revealed, plus it was memorized. Moreover, since science itself relies on evidence to prove any issue, it is reasonable to claim that the Qur'an's preservation is scientific. This is because despite the passage of over fourteen centuries nothing within it violates modern science.

The issue now is merely to determine whether its words conflict with modern science or are in concert with it. Here is a reasonable presumption: if its words contradict modern science, then it is not from God. However, if they agree with it, it must be from Him. Yet, the Qur'an never attempts to prove itself through scientific facts. Thus, its approach is far from apologetic. In fact, it challenges the individual(s) to disprove it. The challenge is that if all of the forces in the universe (literally all of humankind, demons, genies, and spirits, that is every human or human-like force) joined together in an attempt to produce a similar document, they would fail. This is because in contrast to all other books the Qur'an speaks directly to the individual. It is because it specifically provides guidance, focusing upon each individual's needs. This clearly illustrates the fact that its purpose is to provide guidance for humankind, that is for the souls of human beings, rather than for intellectual or scientific inquiry. In other words, the Qur'an seeks to motivate human beings to consider their true origins. Here, humans owe their very existence to almighty God. What's more, it claims that, ultimately, human beings are impotent as power sources. In contrast, God has the mighty power to control all issues. Humans are able to control relatively little. Thus, if He decides upon an event or action, it will happen, regardless of how intensively it is resisted. What's more, with any issue if it is not meant to be, there is nothing anyone can do to force it.

From the Qur'anic perspective even if humans reject the idea of a divine being, a Master and Lord of all, there is a simple fact to recognize: humans are incapable of creating. He alone creates.

The Qur'an is obviously superior to any man-made document. This is because no other document offers its primary attribute, that is the ability to guide human beings. Clearly, the Qur'an alone has this ability. It does so without the need for intercessors, gurus, guides, or priests. While it is helpful for the novice to have an instructor, even so, the instructor merely explains the meaning. It is up to the individual to internalize it as well as act upon it.

Even though the evidence demands that it is divine people may dispute it. They may choose to disbelieve in it. Incredibly, they may even refuse to read it. Yet, such views are not based upon sound reasoning. Rather, such attitudes are largely emotional. In fact, they are based on a kind of prejudice, even hostility, against what is believed to be its message.

Only an inspired work, such as the Qur'an, can ease the pain of a soul or give absolute direction in a time of desperation. The fact is the Qur'an gives guidance upon demand, which is another of its exclusive characteristics.

The Qur'an contains scientific facts, which confirm its "created" origin. Yet, there is little need to prove its source through the sciences. This is because the challenge from its creator is still available, that is for anyone who believes and/or promotes the concept that the Qur'an is man-made, to make another one like it or to even produce a tiny part of it, like a few paragraphs. Since its origin 1400 years ago no one has produced anything similar, that is a document which can inspire and guide human beings to dedicate themselves to almighty God. If there is such a document, a careful scrutiny will reveal its source, which is that it originates ultimately from the Qur'an. The fact is the Qur'an is the only divine text which materially forced a change in civilization. It is the only one which inspired the development of the sciences. Thus, unknowingly, modern civilization reaps uncountable benefits from it. In fact, while never giving credit numerous "New Age" religions utilize it as a basis for their faiths. Thus, a careful scrutiny will determine that if any similar document exists, or even a portion thereof, the Qur'an is its ultimate source. For instance, certain modern Eastern religions claim the oneness of God, even identifying Him as "Allah." Yet, no such concept ever independently developed from either Far Eastern or Western religions. This concept is exclusively Qur'anic, that is only the Qur'an claims that "God is exclusively One." Thus, its contents may be plagiarized. Or, they may be extracted and under other credit rewritten. However, no one has independently produced anything remotely similar to it. This is because it is only the Qur'an which provides the most valuable commodity of all: direct and accurate guidance for the human soul. The fact is if the definition of a miracle is the occurrence of a supernatural or extraterrestrial event, then the Qur'an clearly fits this. Over the centuries people of faith routinely relied upon for their beliefs supernatural phenomena—dramatic miracles, which are impossible for humans to perform or comprehend. The former is the writer's definition, while, similarly, *Webster's Dictionary* defines a miracle as "An event that seems impossible to explain (regarding how it originated)... regarded as supernatural in origin or an act of God (explanation in parenthesis mine)." It also defines it as a thing that inspires "admiration, wonderment, or awe." By this definition the mere existence of the Qur'an represents a miracle, because it is clearly supernatural.

The Qur'an violates the norm. There was no such document and then, suddenly, it arrived. It was a supernatural revelation, delivered directly from God almighty. No human sought it or attempted to create it. Certainly, Muhammad sought no ministry or power through it. Nor did he benefit personally from it. Furthermore, he had nothing to gain from disseminating it, rather, as a result, he endured dire pain and torment. What's more, after he earned power, he continued to live unselfishly, never inciting tyranny. This man had no desire to pursue such a mission, nor to receive any gain. The fact is the Qur'an arose from non-human energies and non-human sources. God Himself decided to send it. The Prophet merely bore it, in other words, he was the agent selected to deliver it. Its purpose is to directly revive humankind. Its source was the vast, hidden heavens. Its recipient was and is the individual human being. Thus, it was an utterly rare event.

Human existence follows certain laws, which are predictable. The Qur'an was unpredictable. Its bearer never expected it. It simply appeared, although systematically.

In normal life nothing is manufactured from a void. The Qur'an seemingly created itself. In other words, it was produced by a type of energy unknown to humans. Call that energy God or whatever it may be called, the fact is the existence of such a document is perhaps the greatest miracle ever known. This is because its origin defies any degree of human explanation. Those who find this reasoning implausible may take the Qur'anic challenge. It claims that no human or group of humans can create its equivalent. True, just how it originated is impossible to explain. Plus, again, the claim that it is from God is a matter of belief. Yet, even so, for such a document to arise someone had to write it. The Qur'an's author challenges any skeptic to produce its equal. No one has even attempted such a project let alone succeeded.

Muhammad was illiterate. Yet, the Qur'an was delivered exclusively through him. There were no Christian or Jewish scholars available for creating it. What's more, it never arose from his followers. Nor did he have a secretive relationship with any writer, scholar, or religious authority. Regarding Christians or Jews they would in any case never have created such a document. This is because it disputes many of their archaic and pagan-derived beliefs. Thus, the Qur'an meets the first part of *Webster's* definition, which is that humans are unable to explain its origin. Furthermore, a review of its contents supports the concept that it is a miracle. This is because it makes a wide range of statements, which have only recently been discovered by modern science. For instance, as late as the 1930s scientists believed that the universe is static, whereas the Qur'an claims it is expanding. The latter is precisely the modern finding. Certainly, such a revelation could never be attributed to an illiterate man, a mere desert inhabitant. Nor can its various profound statements, for instance, 'created humankind from water, made the moon as a source of reflective light, caused the planets/heavenly bodies to float through space in specific orbits, created humankind from mineral muck, created humans systematically in stages, originated life from (stellar) dust, created milk as a filtrate of blood, made (natural) honey as a medicine, etc.' These statements are precise scientific facts, which have been known in the West only since the last 200 years. What's more, many are purely modern discoveries. The fact is it was this book alone which inspired the discoveries of the aforementioned scientific issues. During the early Middle Ages the sciences were unknown. What's more, even the concepts of research and the scientific method were unheard of. Then, the Qur'an arrived. Afterwards, science flourished. While it is true that the ancients produced the beginnings of science, they never finalized them, that is they failed to create the scientific method. It was Islam which created this method. The fact is despite their vast discoveries, even the ancients had no understanding of Qur'anic dictums such as the origin of life from water, mineral muck, and/or stellar dust. This is because they failed to realize that the universe is infinite. As well, during Muhammad's time there was no concept for such primal origins. The fact is such Qur'anic concepts flabbergasted the pagan Arabs. Thus, the contents of the Qur'an itself fully meet *Webster's* second definition for a miracle, i.e. that which inspires "awe and wonderment."

As mentioned previously there is yet another "proof" for the Qur'an's origin. It is the fact that humans are incapable of creating even a small section of it. This is, essentially, irrefutable evidence that its origin is super-

144 Science and Religion

natural. This may explain why no such document has arisen since it was revealed over fourteen centuries ago.

The Qur'an continues with, "God: He alone lives forever, the Master of the Universe. The fact is there is no other god but He." Here, the Qur'an illustrates the true nature of God. It indicates that, like matters of faith, He is permanent. It illustrates that God alone is beyond need. For Him mundane elements—food, water, and rest—are unnecessary. Yet, the claim is He is definitely alive, and His powers are unlimited. It continues with, "It is He Who created the night and day, the sun and the moon. All the celestial bodies float along (in space), each in its own (elliptical) orbit." Not until the 16th and 17th centuries through the works of Brahe and Kepler was it discovered in the West that the planets of the solar system move about in elliptical, that is oval, orbits. Nor did anyone during that era know that the earth or other celestial bodies were mobile. Certainly, the desert dwellers of Arabia had no access to scholarly works. Furthermore, even if they did they had no means to understand them. What's more, the ancients never mentioned this specific attribute, this floating of huge planets as they bob along in their orbits.

Let us revisit such words to comprehend their impact. During such an early era no human could have known this. Even in early modern astronomy this concept of "floating through space" is unknown. To confirm this a search can be made of all astronomy textbooks from the early part of this century to the 1950's, when the bases for the current beliefs were established. No such statements will be found. Thus, the only possible conclusion is that the Qur'an, this seventh century revelation, like all other true revelations, has as its source a purely non-human entity. Certainly, an individual may choose not to believe in it. Yet, the fact is only an almighty God, who truly comprehends the mechanisms which control this phenomenally vast and complicated universe, could be its source. Certainly, no human could have written it, nor could any scholar or group of scholars write it today. Thus, what other source could there be other than God?

While it is little appreciated, much of modern astronomy has its origin in Islam. Regarding the early Muslims the Qur'an created a fascination for this science. The findings of the movement of the great spheres were well known to Islamic astronomers. During the 10th century, which was the height of Islamic astronomical discoveries, Muslim scholars made observations of the heavenly bodies which were highly accurate. According to Western historians their measurements were so precise that they are essentially modern. In fact, in their study of the universe modern astronomers utilize these measurements. Yet, in today's history books credit for the discovery of modern astronomy is never attributed to the Muslims.

In the 12th century Muslim astronomers in Spain discovered that rather than being circular planetary orbits are elliptical, that is oval. Today's astronomy books claim that this discovery completely revolutionized astronomy and may be the most important astronomical discovery ever. Yet, full credit for this crucial finding, that is that the orbits of the planets in the solar system are oval, is routinely attributed to Western scientists. However, in scholarly books, such as the *Dictionary of Scientific Biography* and the *Encyclopedia of the History of Arabic Science*, the European claim for such discoveries has been disputed. For instance, in Islamic Spain during the 12th century A.D. az-Zarqali and other scholars described the orbits of the planets as elliptical (i.e. oval), categorically noting, for example, that the orbit of mercury is "an ellipse." Such revolutionary comments influenced the thinking of European scholars, that is after the books of Islamic astronomers were translated into Latin. The fact is Copernicus himself claimed to be heavily indebted to Arabic/Islamic scholars for his planetary theories, as was Kepler, to whom the discovery of the ellipse is apparently wrongly credited. Kepler relied extensively upon Islamic scientists, who he regarded as his "ancient fathers," a term also coined by Copernicus. Also, incredibly, Copernicus was an amateur astronomer, who derived his ideas regarding the solar system from Islamic books. He conducted no

---

[1] For more information regarding the history of modern science see Dr. Khaleel's book, *The True Origins of Modern Science* (Knowledge House, 2003). To order call 1-800-243-5242 or check the website, www.knowledgehousepublishers.com

scientific experiments. What's more, to the original Islamic scholars the works of Copernicus would have been regarded as inconsequential, because he based his views solely upon theories, whereas Muslim astronomers proved their theories through scientific experiments. It was Briffault who, in his book, *Rational Evolution*, claimed that were it not for the Islamic astronomers "there would have been no Copernicus." Therefore, the highly rational and detail-oriented Muslim astronomers, such as Ibn al-Haytham, Ibn ash-Shatir, al-Battani, az-Zarqali, and numerous others, must, through the definition established by European and American historians, be regarded as the true founders of precision and experimental astronomy.[1]

Interestingly, according to Thomas Welty Islamic astronomers knew the earth was a globe. What's more, their knowledge of heavenly bodies was so advanced that according to Will Durant discoveries which European astronomers took great pride in, such as the fact that the earth rotates and planets orbit, were "taken for granted," that is they were elementary knowledge. This may have been aided by the fact that the Arabic word in the Qur'an describing the earth, that is *dahaha*, means "egg shaped." Interestingly, the fact that the earth is oval, rather, egg shaped, was only recently discovered, that is during the 20th century. Yet, as early as the seventh century Muslim astronomers realized this. In addition, as early as the ninth century Muslim scholars were fully aware that the earth rotates on its axis, a finding which was utterly unknown in Europe. In contrast, in medieval Europe anyone who promoted such a concept was regarded as a heretic. What's more, the mere mention of an infinite universe led to imprisonment and/or death. This caused innumerable scholars to study only in hiding. Indeed, until the 18th century scientists and other scholars throughout Europe, as well as England, were persecuted for presenting the truths of science.

During the medieval era the Church vehemently fought the advancement of science. It created specific laws against the study of non-clerical works. No knowledge could be pursued without church approval. The consequences of such scrutiny were dire. When scholars attempted to educate the masses, the agents of the Church persecuted them. For instance, anyone who discounted the official claim that the earth was flat or that it was the center of the universe was vilified, perhaps murdered. Special squadrons were created to hunt for and punish scholars. The scientists endured every conceivable form of indignity, from torture and imprisonment to death by torture, decapitation, hanging, disembowelment, or burning at the stake. The sciences, which were responsible for the advancement of civilization, could never have developed in such an environment. Thus, the current concept that this modern civilization is Judeo-Christian in origin is utterly false. Rather, the opposite is true, that is Western powers obstructed the growth of the sciences and, therefore, civilization. It was Islam alone which created modern science and civilization. It alone encouraged scientific enterprise. It exclusively promoted intellectual interchange between all cultures. True, Christians and to a lesser degree Jews assisted in this process, however, this was entirely under the auspices of Islam. Recent analysis documents that during the Middle Ages fully 95% of the books produced, tens of thousands of volumes, were written by Muslims.

Yet, Islam was always the progenitor of a balanced, progressive civilization. This is because it created the environment for massive growth. It was the true benefactor, because it financially supported scientific achievement. During the Islamic Era the state treasury was spent primarily for education and public works. Thus, as a system it fully supported the pursuit of learning. Islam produced the world's first public school system, after which today's system is modeled. What's more, it encouraged, in fact, initiated, international as well as interdenominational studies.

Islam accepts the beliefs of all who recognize almighty God. No other system does so. This is why it alone caused the flourishing of civilization. It is also why it will do so in the future. In contrast, the Jews fail to accept the Christians as true, even though, incredibly, they worship from the same book. Nor do the Christians accept Judaism as a correct faith. Islam recognizes all monotheistic faiths as well as their prophets: without question. In contrast, Christianity and Judaism fail to accept Muhammad's prophethood. This is true, even though he preached precisely the same messages as Moses and Jesus. Thus, there is seemingly no reasonable reason to fail to recognize him. The fact is by accepting him Christians and Jews receive the most up-to-date information regarding the faith. They gain the advantage of a written history of the rules of God versus oral traditions, upon which they are now dependent. Thus, they receive direct access to vibrant, invaluable information: life-changing revelation versus revelation contaminated with pagan rites. They receive a practical type of revelation, which is readily and systematically applied in daily life. Yet, even so, the Bible is a phenomenal book, which has guided countless individuals over the centuries. It contains invaluable principles, which many have applied to improve and guide their lives. The problem is sorting out the true from the false, that is the divine from the man-made.

This issue is worth exploring, that is the attempt to exclude the Prophet Muhammad as a legitimate messenger. Is his message possibly a threat to certain forces? Through misinformation are people being driven away from the valuable wisdom he offers? Certainly, historically, there is no reason to exclude him. After all, Moses, Jesus, and Muhammad are direct descendants of the same father: the Prophet Abraham. Thus, they all possess the same genes. Virtually everyone recognizes Abraham. All are willing to admit this tie. Common sense would indicate that all who come from him are of the same status, the same essence. To exclude any one of them would be highly biased. So, could there be any confusion regarding the last from this chain, that is the Prophet Muhammad? In some circles, that is the orthodox Christians and Jews, of all the prophets originating from Abraham he alone is excluded. Incredibly, he alone is deemed a false prophet. Only he is the victim of a vast propaganda campaign. Why are doubts circulated regarding his authenticity? Perhaps it is a racial issue. Yet, the Prophet himself never associated with a race. The fact is when he was questioned about being an Arab, he rejected any such association. Rather, he described himself as a servant of God, that is his agent and messenger. Thus, he never emphasized his lineage. People might picture him as an 'Arab' (of the desert). Yet, history proves his message was universal. The fact is he described himself as an agent of God sent not for the benefit of the few but for all humankind.

Incredibly, in the West Jesus is pictured as 'white', in fact, Northern European. Yet, assuredly he was dark complected, since he was purely of Middle Eastern blood. Plus, he lived in a sunny climate. The fact is Jesus' blood line or the blood line of Moses has never been a hindrance in believing in him. Plus, regarding the authenticity of his mission no one doubts it. Yet, many people fail to realize that all the major prophets, including the Prophet Muhammad, are from this same blood line. All preached the same message. The statements of the major prophets, Noah, Abraham, Moses, Jesus, and

Muhammad, are virtually identical. All preached belief in the one and only God along with belief in life after death. All fought against evil and tyranny. All emphasized the love and compassion of God. Yet, in the case of many Westerners only the Prophet Muhammad is excluded. This exclusion may simply be due to a lack of information. Yet, this is a vast loss, because his preaching is by far the most complete. It is also the most well preserved. No one knows for certain the exact color of Jesus' skin or for that matter any other prophet. However, what is certain is that he couldn't have been stark white, as the images denote, otherwise, he would have become burnt from the hot desert sun. Even so, color is of no consequence regarding the true nature of a person. It is what is within the heart that matters. Incredibly, modern science today proves the human race is contiguous. In other words, all people are of mixed genes. All are genetically related. Thus, there is no "pure race." Furthermore, a high percentage of today's inhabitants—billions of people—are direct descendants from Abraham and are, therefore, brothers and sisters in faith. What's more, through the Virgin Mary Jesus is a direct descendant of Abraham, so is Muhammad. Thus, Jesus and Muhammad, both descendants of Abraham, are brothers in faith.

From the Qur'anic point of view a superior race is unknown. Superiority is based solely upon the level of an individual's faith as well as his degree of knowledge. Thus, the view of Islam is simplistic: the level of faith and dedication to God are the only issues which distinguish the individual. Any other attempt to qualify or categorize a person is a rebellion against its principles and is, in fact, criminal. Thus, to exert authority over people because of tribal status, race, wealth, or political power is its very antithesis. In fact, it is evidence of disbelief.

Yet, sadly, during the Middle Ages the Church failed to adopt such principles. Driven by greed and dogmatic beliefs it proved relentless. The Inquisition was so comprehensive that no one was immune. It was in the West where men of learning, such as Galileo, were obstructed from pursuing the sciences. The fact is Galileo was forced "over the Bible" to renounce his lifelong works on planetary motion. He was imprisoned and subjected to abuses. Incredibly, during the 16th century Bruno was burned at the stake for the crime of claiming that the earth rotates about its axis. What's more, certain European scholars, such as England's Roger Bacon, were tabbed "satanic Muslims" because of their endeavors to pursue the sciences. Roger Bacon, who should be largely credited for bringing the sciences to England, was imprisoned for some 17 years. Thus, in every conceivable way Western powers delayed, in fact, obstructed the development of the sciences, while Islam accelerated it. Bruno and Bacon were Christians, who devoted their all against great odds for the advancement of the sciences. Yet, whether scholar, prisoner of war, or civilian in liberal Islam torture of the innocent was unknown. No one was burned at the stake. Barbarism was never Islam's. Rather, it was always its victim. Yet, this is far from a single person's opinion. Historical texts agree that under Islam's original system, which flourished for nearly seven centuries, scientists were given total freedom: no one was tortured or killed for their beliefs. This environment of relative peace led to a massive scientific movement. While Islam achieved the pinnacle of sophistication, Europe fell to the lowest level of barbarism. This is because the latter deliberately thwarted intellectual progress. Europe was in a quagmire. It required a savior. That savior was Islam.

Educated by the Qur'an, the Muslim rulers were drawn to the sciences. This was because this text provides insight to its followers, causing them to search for astronomical, as well as biological, truths. It clearly describes the planets as moving spheres and how they proceed methodically in their orbits. Furthermore, the existence of the various planets of this solar system is hinted with, "We have created beyond you (several) celestial orbits (one after the other)." Here, the Qur'an makes it clear that there exist numerous planets near the earth. Such Qur'anic dictums clearly illustrate why Islamic civilization supported the sciences. Thus, it is no surprise that while during the Middle Ages European rulers killed or imprisoned their astronomers, Islamic rulers awarded theirs with prizes of gold and silver as well as positions of honor.

There is no peace today. Hundreds of nations are embroiled in futile wars. What's more, they are also the victims of economic wars. Yet, other wars are being waged such as the war against the human mind. People's minds are under siege from a variety of evils. Certainly, there is little opportunity for the flourishing of intellect. The distractions are overpowering. A focus on mental advancement is rarely emphasized. People are consumed in prurient pursuits, and they have no means to escape. Islam offers the ability to create such stability. Thus, it should be thoroughly investigated to determine its true worth, that is the rules and principles it provides, for the creation of a stable, peaceful, and sophisticated world.

Scientific proofs: a Qur'anic Concept

As mentioned previously this is an orderly universe. This earth has existed in perfect order for billions of years. It has never deviated from its rotation or orbit. It is consistently nourished by the sun and balanced, gravitationally, by the moon. This degree of precision dominates the entire universe, as stated in the Qur'an: "Are you unaware of how God created the (numerous) layers of the universe in absolute harmony?" What's more, regarding His controlling influence, "and We are (involved in and) fully aware of (all aspects of) Our creation."

We again find: "To Him is due the primal origin of the heavens and the earth. When He decrees a matter, He merely says 'Be' and it is." This demonstrates the unfathomable and infinitely great powers of the almighty Lord. It indicates that whatever God wills He merely commands it, and it happens. It is a type of self-proclamation, which only a most magnificent creature, one beyond human comprehension, can make, that is the ability to originate something from nothing, without any effort. Thus, Islam suggests that even the creation of the heavens and the earth was a minor task for God and that He failed to require, as is popularly believed, an additional day for rest. The Qur'an also states: "We have created all things by pairs (i.e. opposites), that perhaps you may (truly) consider it." Objects of this world, as well as in the vast universe, exist in a paired form. Animals and plants are most often bisexual. In plants the stamen and pistil unite to form a wedded pair. Genes themselves also exist in pairs, allele to allele. Even inanimate phenomena, such as rock crystals and electricity, as well as the atom (i.e. protons and electrons), are based on a paired existence. On a more profound level recent findings indicate that stars have pairs, huge celestial bodies, which orbit them every few thousand years. These are called binary systems. The sun may have such a pair, although it has never been definitively known. The earth itself is paired, that is with the moon. Yet, there is another more personal pair indicated by the Qur'an: the pair of personalities, that is the two sides of each person, good and evil, loving and angry, peaceful and hateful, happy and sad. It is the two sides of the human soul, the good and positive versus the dark and diabolical. Ultimately, it is the two souls, the living one and the one that goes on into the next existence.

The Qur'an also states: "the heavens and the earth were at first one mass; then, We exploded it, and (ultimately) created every living thing from water." This hints at the methodical and prolonged development of the universe, which scientists have fully proven. What's more, the sequence of the events is notable. The issue of water is mentioned only after describing the original galactic explosion. Such an explosion created and released the very basis of all existence: the atomic material, that is the electrons, protons, and neutrons. Ultimately, this became the element hydrogen. Science has proven that this element forms the basis of all matter, including water molecules. Astronomers maintain that the universe began as a single highly condensed mass of matter, which was somehow broken apart. The Big Bang theory suggests a massive cosmic explosion. It is also agreed that this matter eventually gave rise to the universe, its heavenly bodies, and ultimately, all living beings. The words "We created every living thing from water" corresponds to only the latest knowledge in biology. Water is the dominant life-sustaining fluid; "...He it is that created human beings from water." The fact that 70% of the human body consists of water would be elementary knowledge to God. Perhaps even more profoundly the Qur'an delves (section six) into the possible primal origin of life with, "...it is He who created you (originally) from one living entity." This is exclusively a 20th century discovery. Yet, there is no elaboration of just what that entity was. Thus, it is left to the imagination. Nor, is there any indication of how long it took for humankind to develop as a viable creation. Yet, this statement fuels the speculation that life on this earth began as a single cell, which multiplied, ultimately leading to various life-forms.

What is perhaps even more astounding are the implications of a preceding statement found in the same Qur'anic section, which implies that 'God has created stellar material as the basis of life.' Today, scientists regard this material as the molecular basis of all existence, including human life. Stellar dust is, essentially, the atomic fuel, as it were, which energizes the universe and was ultimately formed into the atoms and molecules that humans are made of. It is the mass which forms the basis of all that exists. The atom, which is the ultimate building block for all that exists, originates in stellar dust. Thus, this molecular source for all matter is precisely mentioned in the Qur'an. What's more, according to Preston Cloud this very earth, as well as the sun, originated from such dust. The watery origin of living beings is directly tied with stellar dust, since the latter is the original source of hydrogen, of which water is largely made. Oxygen, the other component of water, is also thought to have developed from hydrogen. Dust particles in outer space have been proven to contain water as ice crystals. Here is one theory for how water formed. In the explosive environment of space water vapor was eventually created. This crystallized as ice. This ice is thought to have condensed within heavenly bodies, ultimately, under extreme pressure, melting into water. The water then came out through vents and through volcanoes as steam. It re-condensed, forming lakes and oceans. Yet, stellar hydrogen is believed to be the source for the electrons from which water, including the water we drink, is made. In fact, all that exists appears to have originated from this simple atom. Thus, through these Qur'anic proofs He reminds humans of the modest origin for all creation, including human beings. In other words, even water, the life-giving fluid, which humans are completely dependent upon, has a simplistic origin. Yet, how is it that He created water out of "dust"? That is the fascinating aspect of the divine capacity—that divine wisdom— which humans find unfathomable. What's more, the implication is that all that exists, living or non-living, originated from the radioactive wispy dust, which floats through the midst of space. This is precisely the modern finding. Robert Jastrow claims in his book, *God and the Astronomers*, that the universe began as a massive explosion, liberating vast quantities of cosmic dust. Cloud, in his book *Oasis in Space*, says that this dust was eventually condensed to form heavenly bodies, including the earth. He confirms the Qur'anic view, that all life originated from this dust. Some of this dust still exists and is apparently billions of years old. It not only contains hydrogen and helium but, in fact, often contains water molecules, in the form of ice.

This ancient dust is very radioactive. In fact, it is so radioactive that it would destroy any life exposed to it. Yet, in a way unknown to humans both the earth, as well as our human bodies, originate from it. Jastrow claims that eons ago the universe contained exclusively hydrogen and that humans owe their existence to it. It is an amazing design. All began with a simple atom, which became diversified into hundreds of others. What is most incredible is the fact that these seemingly dead or inert molecules ultimately are transformed into living beings. This is precisely the point of view presented in the Qur'an. Yet, just how substances which are so utterly toxic—radioactive ions—could develop into the very essence of life: oxygen and water, remains unknown. Even more unfathomable is the fact that these naturally radioactive molecules are ultimately converted into living beings, for instance, humans. How could they become so metamorphosized to create life? How can substances so toxic that merely touching them can kill then lead to the living? Certainly, it is a feat humans are unable to comprehend, let alone achieve. In other words, no scientist, rather, not even legions of them, can possibly explain the mechanism. Scientists fully agree upon this mechanism, however, they have no clue how it occurred. Yet, from Islam's point of view it is God who did it. No further explanation is required.

This type of design, this conversion of universal chaos—the chaos of radioactive atoms—into organized matter: that alone is a monumental feat. However, then for these molecules to be specifically geared for the creation of living beings, such a system could only arise through a careful plan. In other words, it all had to begin with an idea. This implies that there must exist an Idea-Maker. In contrast, when humans create radioactivity, for instance, an atomic bomb or medical radiation, it only destroys. It causes only death: never life. Yet, the universal radiation, which is seemingly equally dangerous as the man-made type, is the basis of all living beings? Is there any other option besides the fact that a great and merciful God is responsible? Who else could turn radioactive molecules into living beings? In contrast, when humans experiment with radiation all they can create are mutations, never life. This creation of beings from radioactive molecules belongs exclusively to an extraterrestrial domain, that is the domain of almighty God.

Certainly, this view of the universe is the opposite of Darwin's theories, which claim that everything arises by chance. Yet, a thorough study of the universe reveals that Darwin's theories are erroneous. The universe operates completely by plan. What's more, it is permeated by a specific Force, which obviously plans and manages all creation. It would be a Force, in fact, a Being, of such might that it is beyond imagination. It is the Being that knew in advance what would ultimately develop. Too, it is a Being of indescribable compassion: the all-merciful, almighty God. In other words, it is a Being who loves His creation so dearly that He created the very molecules needed for survival. Only such a Being could convert chaos and confusion, i.e. the chaos of universal clouds of radioactive dust, into the very basis of biological existence. This is an incredible feat: to convert the most toxic, radioactive substances known into, ultimately, living flesh. Could such organization of matter, such a specific, viable plan, arise from any other source, that is other than God? The fact is there is no other answer, despite any attempt to the contrary. This is clear evidence that an all-knowing Being exists, who exhibits love, as well as forethought, for creation. It is also proof for the presence of a Being of unfathomable intelligence as well as power. Those simple molecules, oxygen and water, how incredibly divine, both in design and source, they are. Human beings may take this for granted. Yet, all humans are utterly dependent upon them. Every breath each person takes and every sip of water he consumes: all are gifts from almighty God.

The Qur'anic view is that God's synthetic factory produced all that exists and all that humans are dependent upon. Water molecules, oxygen, solar rays, the various species, the bountiful produce: all are His. Is there any other power to recognize or thank besides Him?

Also within the aforementioned Qur'anic section the unfathomable state of darkness, which permeates outer space, is described as a type of "frightening darkness." Using the imagination what could be more dark, the depths of that primal soup, that is layer upon layer of muck, where life began, or the deep darkness of the primordial oceans, depth upon depth, or even more frightening, the dark, treacherous recesses of outer space? In what is typical of the Qur'an's mind-torquing parables the moral appears to be that without the brilliant light of divine guidance and the magnificence of divine support humankind founders: in the darkness of the mind and spirit, in the darkness and confusion of its own soul. Yet, perhaps, too, it could imply that humanity is at risk for loss from that darkness of the passage: death. Yet, regarding that ultimate event it is the darkness of failing to prepare for its inevitability, while realizing it.

The absurdity of certain concepts promulgated by people of faith has fueled the conflict between religion and science. It also explains why scientists have rejected the validity of revelation. The idea that the universe is very young, that is less than 6,000 years old, as some people claim, creates great skepticism towards religion. Still, people adamantly espouse this belief, one that defies common sense and is easily disproved. The "six day" belief has led to a loss in credibility. True, certain adherents maintain that scripture must be interpreted literally, particularly the Bible. Thus, for such individuals if the Bible says that the universe and/or the earth were created in six days, it means precisely that: six 24 hour periods. The view may be sincere, since it is based upon the desire to resolutely obey the divinity. However, usually, there is no allowance for interpretation. What's more, incredibly, the use of reason is never considered.

Certain archaic translations of the Qur'an may also imply such a meaning.

This short-phase creation is completely implausible. The fossil record alone dispels such an idea. Yet, this is far from an attempt to disparage the Bible: God did create the earth over a period of days: His days. What's more, is it reasonable to presume that anyone with the kind of Power capable of creating the vast universe, with its untold billions of star-laden galaxies and its innumerable life forms—could such a Being become so exhausted as to be forced to rest, that is to collapse in fatigue? The fact is if such an ever-present and all-controlling creator tired easily, what would happen to the universe if He fell asleep at those monumental controls or if He became so exhausted that He lost focus and made a major error? If an all-powerful Master of the Universe exists, the idea that He needs rest fails to compute. If He is all-powerful, He is powerful enough not to need rest.

Think about it. If we become tired or fall asleep, whatever is dependent upon our actions must cease. Who will maintain such a job while we sleep? Would this be any different for the Master of all? What about the creation of what is infinitely more vast: an entire galaxy containing billions upon billions of stars, in fact, billions of such galaxies? Is there any evidence that this depleted or exhausted Him? The workers at Chernobyl lapsed into fatigue, causing a reactor to explode in an utter catastrophe. A single error caused damage of such a massive degree that it is immeasurable. What about the untold billions of nuclear "reactors" under God almighty's control? If, then, the rules that apply for this earth also apply for the universe, the slightest lapse, that is the least bit of fatigue or the minutest loss in focus, could lead to a monumental catastrophe, perhaps the universe's annihilation. Or, is this concept of the requirement by God of rest merely a human creation meant to establish a day of rest from the daily bread: the origin of Sunday? In other words, humans felt the need for rest, so they invented a law and attribute it to Him. In section 50 the Qur'an views this issue differently, for instance, "(The fact is) We created the vast universe and the earth, as well as all that is between, in six eons. What's more, We never tired in the least during the process." The Arabic word, *yawm*, translated literally as "day," actually means a potentially long or unpredictably long time. It may mean an unending number of days, months, or years, that is forever. However, it may also mean a single day or several days. Even so, the Qur'an leaves no doubt regarding the lengthy nature of creation, claiming, symbolically, that one of almighty God's days is exceptionally long i.e. "50,000 human days." Thus, incredibly, a day in the divine realm is equal to some 132 human years. This means that a divine year equals over 48,000 years. This is longer than all written history. An entire dynasty, such as the time of the Pharaohs, is a mere 5,000 human years old. Yet, in God's eyes this is only days, in fact, little more than a month.

The word six itself as used in the Qur'an is largely symbolic. It may be interpreted as "numerous," that is numerous millennia, numerous infinitely long eons, perhaps a billion years or more long, or whatever time span such a magnificent Creator uses to measure the vastness of universal time. Perhaps it truly means six, that is six of God's time measurements. The Arabic indicates that this represents six infinitely long periods of time, which are beyond human comprehension. Certainly, it could indicate six geological eons, that is 6 billion years. This may well be correct. Regarding the age of the earth it cannot be determined with certainty. The estimate is that it is about 4 billion years old. This represents the time that the actual earth and solar system formed. Yet, it took time for the elements that are the basis of the solar system, that is the stellar dust and molecules, to form. Perhaps this represents an additional 2 billion years. This would equal the Qur'anic amount. While only further research will tell, the possibility exists that certain elements within the earth or the remainder of the solar system could well be 6 billion years old.

Obviously, it is implausible that in the seventh century pagan Arabs could readily understand such massive perceptions of time. The fact is in that region the entire concept of time was unknown. What's more, it is likely that the concept of six was used in the Qur'an as a reference point for the prevailing beliefs of previous scriptures. In other words, the Qur'an sought to avoid creating a new idea, since people of previous scriptures would vehemently resist it. It was perhaps also used to refute the fact that a "day" of rest, that is the so-called seventh day, of Christian lore was for such a divine power unnecessary.

The Qur'an's objective is to attempt to make sense of the essentially unfathomable concept of creation and of universal time, that is for anyone willing to use his/her common sense. It attempts to remind people of the vast and unfathomable powers of almighty God as well as the humbleness of human origins. It seeks to bring everyone into its fold, that is into the arena of submission of the self—submission of the heart and soul—to almighty God.

Yet, all this is merely an attempt to jostle human minds and to stimulate reasoning. It is to cause humans to think for a singular purpose. It is so that people will make the essential decision, to believe or not to believe, to be grateful or remain indifferent or even ungrateful. It is an attempt to remind humans of their humble origins. Thus, according to the Qur'an human beings have a rather lowly origin: mere mineral matter. In its view the original source for whatever exists in the universe, including human beings, is a type of dust: stellar dust. Watery or wet mineral matter as a source has also been mentioned. Thus, essentially, as described in the Qur'an in sections 23 and 32 humans originate from a type of mud, a muck-like "clay." The definition of clay is that it is a type of mineral-rich, water-impregnated muck. Such a muck would contain all of the components necessary for life: water, minerals, and even trapped oxygen.

Notably, the Qur'an didn't mention dirt, that is soil, as the source. This makes sense, because from a chemical point of view the latter is relatively low in minerals and high in organic matter. In contrast, clay is the ancient compaction from the decomposition of mineral-rich rock. It is essentially water-soluble rock, which is literally billions of years old, a sort of rock soup. Yet, incredibly, upon looking at it clay has no appearance of a mineral origin. Thus, the parable may relate to its molecular/atomic nature, that is a water-mineral mix. This along with the previous statement regarding the watery origins clearly indicates that water is key to the genesis of life. So are minerals, which are the spark plugs for cellular growth. However, the minerals must be in a certain state, in a clay-like consistency, that is a water soluble form, for life to be generated. This is the form mentioned directly in the Qur'an.

According to modern science life is dependent upon enzymes. These enzymes can only operate in a watery environment. What's more, minerals are required to activate them. Without minerals, enzymes are rendered inactive. Water is required to activate both minerals and enzymes.

The importance of this water-mineral mix is indicated through the mention of a clay-like substance, found in sections 15, 23, and 32. Thus, regarding how life originated the Qur'an provides a significant clue. In fact, it indicates that the scientific theory of the primeval soup may well be correct. It does so because the implication is that mineral matter by itself fails to support life. However, when it is mixed with fluid, that is water, it becomes the muck that sustains life, perhaps creates it.

A literal translation of such passages may prove misleading. Here, clay could be viewed as something to be molded into a specific shape. Interestingly, translations vary with the intellectual capacity of the translator(s). This capacity is dependent upon the time in history as well as the depth of faith of the translator. While a thorough knowledge of the native language, in this case, Arabic, is required, incredibly, the insight, that is the faith and commitment, is even more important. A person who has a perfect understanding of Arabic and English but who lacks moral fiber will fail to properly translate this text, in fact, the reverse, that is a distorted translation, will result. This is because a mind distorted in its understanding of God could never properly translate His text. In other words, God guides only those who will to be guided, that is those who make the effort to believe in Him. This may explain the deficiencies in many existing translations. Thus, for instance previous translators have presumed that, since clay is plastic and can be molded, somehow, God designed human beings from it. God perhaps molded it until He determined the shape He desired, then fired it into its final form in His "kiln." The Christian point of view is similar. According to traditional thinking from this original "male" God took a rib to make the female. The fact is it is now known that this story is purely a fable.

This is the way much of the Bible is translated. However, an accurate reading of the Qur'an provides a more basic view. In the human species like all others God created both males and females: period.

In literal translations, whether biblical or Qur'anic, the true meaning is usually missed. For instance, regarding the issue of clay the orthodox translators had no understanding of its chemical nature. They failed to consider the fact that it is mineral matter. They were unable to comprehend that when it is mixed with water, it becomes mineral muck, which is similar to the type of material that life originated in. They had no understanding that only in this form—this water-soluble clay—can earthen minerals create life. What's more, a literal interpretation belies the actual meaning of the Arabic term that is used when describing creation, which indicates the occurrence of a type of transmutation, an evolution of sorts, where life gradually developed, where human beings resulted, gradually. Such a process would require both minerals and water in a soluble form, i.e. clay.

Thus, the Qur'an uses a terminology which indicates that humans originated from this mineral muck through a type of transformation, one stage to the next. The fact is throughout it the creation of humans is described as a step-wise, gradual process. Yet, this is far from a proclamation that God made humans from a specific lower creature, for instance, apes. There is no evidence for such a claim. That is merely a theory. However, the Qur'an makes it clear that human life originated in a watery environment, that is a mineral-rich mud. From its position this is all that is known. Precisely how human beings developed, or, for that matter, any of the other diverse species, remains unknown. Yet, what is clear is that life originated and is also sustained through a mineral-enriched watery environment. Yet, merely hard minerals plus water, like particles of gravel or sand in water, won't suffice. A crude muck, i.e. "clay," is required to sustain life.

Science confirms this. This is because without water and minerals, together, the creation of life, at least as it is understood today, is impossible. Every scientist knows that any region or planet which lacks water is unable to support life of any kind: period. The Qur'an agrees with this, since it categorically states that all life is created from water. This would indicate that throughout this vast universe or on this earth without water all is sterile. The example of when water is lacking on this earth makes this evident. Drought causes certain regions to lose all forms of life, even where it once flourished. According to the Prophet Muhammad drought will ultimately cause the earth's destruction. To counter this he recommended the aggressive planting of trees. This drought will likely be caused by damage to the atmosphere through pollution. It may also be caused by the constant contamination of the earth by toxic chemicals, which sterilize plant life. If the atmosphere is irreparably damaged, the danger is that the ozone and water vapor will be lost into space. In other words, much of the protective powers of the atmosphere's structure will be lost, plus the loss of water vapor could lead to catastrophic drought. Only future research will tell the degree of danger this will cause. However, trees produce vast amounts of oxygen, and this may explain the Prophet's futuristic comments, since the earthly oxygen, that is the oxygen made by plant life, is the source of the protective ozone.

Modern science presented the theory of the watery origins of life only through intensive study and research. The purpose of mentioning it in the Qur'an is primarily to remind human beings of their simple origins, that is to motivate them to consider these origins, so they will be grateful. It is so they will remain truly humble in their hearts. It is so they will never allow themselves to become arrogant and, therefore, self-destructive. It is so they will realize that arrogance and self-righteousness are violations of the true human nature, characteristics which, ultimately, will cause the destruction of both humanity and this earth. Human arrogance will ultimately cause civilization's doom. Every existing scripture predicts this result. Could they all be in error?

This humble origin of humankind is the major reason for the description of the watery and mineral origin of life. Yet, the mention of such an origin could be misconstrued as an attempt by the Qur'an to confirm human evolution from lower creatures. It might even be perceived as evidence that men arose directly from animals, that is apes. However, the Qur'an indicates otherwise, claiming that God created the human being of a high status, infusing him with a profound and elegant essence. In fact, it describes him as a separate and unique creation, unrelated to the lower animals. Regarding the details of the precise origins of humans none are available. True, Islam confirms the ancient watery beginning of life, for humankind as well as all other life forms. In fact, this origin of all life from water was from a scientific point of view first popularized by Muslim scholars. It was the Islamic scholars, Ibn Sina (10th century) as well as al-Biruni (11th century), who first noted the watery origins of life. They discovered this by studying fossil-laden sedimentary rock. Yet, even for evolutionists the precise nature of how humans developed remains unknown. Fossilized bones alone are incapable of explaining the origin of such a refined, intelligent being.

Thus, a watery origin for life implies that all life originated from two simple atoms: hydrogen and oxygen. It indicates that without the availability of the simplest of all substances, water molecules, there would be no life. It implies that if God withdrew that blessing, that is halted the delivery or production of water, all would die. Regarding the possibility or method by which one form of life became transmuted into another, that is the modern theory of evolution, no information is provided. Rather, the indication if any is that all life forms have been specifically created, made from life-giving raw materials such as water, minerals, organic material and, ultimately, stellar dust. Precisely how this happened remains a mystery.

These futuristic Qur'anic dictums make it evident why of all religions Islam is devoid of hostility toward the sciences. Some religions regard material achievements as a hindrance to the soul. The Islamic position is to the contrary, since it is mandatory for Muslims to seek knowledge in all areas. It is also their duty to become as successful in any endeavor as possible. Thus, from the Islamic point of view to gain knowledge is an obligation just as critical in importance, in fact, more critical, than attending worship services. A lack of learning is tantamount to a deficiency in commitment. This learning is both for spiritual and practical, that is scientific, endeavors. Thus, Islam requires the pursuit of material achievements. This means that the creation of material advancements, that is advancements which will facilitate the growth and development of civilization, is a divine obligation. The fact is there is a greater obligation to improve society, in other words, to create valuable material achievements, than mere religious scholarship. This is because the objective of Islam is rather simplistic: the productive service of humanity. Without service, without the labor to make this world a superior place, Islam serves no function. Otherwise, it is relegated to mundane ritual. Otherwise, it is merely a religion like all others.

Islam was great when it created greatness, that is in the material world. It was superior when it produced achievements for the sake of humanity. It was superior when it rescued humans from pagan, self-destructive ways to the way of almighty God. Islam means social and human advancement. There is no other interpretation for it.

Yet, it cannot be claimed that Islam is no longer a contributor. This is because it is precisely the source of modern science, a fact thoroughly documented by Western historians. Nor can it be claimed that "Muslims" are merely "taking advantage" of Western institutions. The fact is Islam created the scientific method. Thus, it is the West which is the opportunist, because it fails to credit the Islamic source. Despite this the media frequently creates the impression that Muslims or "Arabs" are opportunists, merely taking advantage of Western technology. In other words, the impression is only the West has created civilization and science, while Islam is dependent upon it. This is an utter distortion. The fact is algebra, arithmetic, medicine, pharmacology, physics, geology, chemistry, and astronomy, while seemingly Western in appearance, are Islamic in origin. The fact is a thorough evaluation determines the presence of Islam in all arenas. Therefore, Muslims who go to school in America, whether citizens or immigrants, must have at least equal share in the glory of Western institutions. The fact is they deserve a greater share, because who deserves the most credit, the originator or the follower?

For religion to be beneficial there must be a thirst for self-improvement. There must also exist a desire to grow freely in knowledge. Otherwise, it becomes a tedious practice, one which is usually avoided, neglected, or even despised. In its true condition instead of being a religion Islam is a movement, a positive vital force. It is that force stimulating the achievement of the highest degree of success, both in this life and the next. It is the most dynamic system for creating a balanced, just civilization. It is the most reliable method for ensuring that the earth and its inhabitants develop, as well as flourish, in the most healthy, productive, and positive way possible. It is the essential means for preventing human tyranny, both toward the fellow man and this very planet.

As mentioned previously Islam is defined as subjugation of personal desires for the desires of almighty God. What's more, it is a willing subjugation. If it is done with resistance, that is not "Islam." Therefore, to be a "Muslim," i.e. one who willingly submits, a degree of understanding must be developed. Without understanding, without the careful, methodical use of reason, there is no Islam even if it appears superficially so. The fact is it is impossible for an unlearned person to truly understand the attributes of a wise and intelligent God. This is the God of Islam, the God also known as Allah. The question is regarding this submission, what are God's primary requirements? The first word revealed in the Qur'an was "Read," that is "use your intellect." Imagine the implications: of all possible words only read was selected. Nothing was said about religious sacrifice, self-denial, or becoming "holy." Thus, the Qur'an fails to urge the pursuit of spirituality or asceticism. Rather, its approach is to use the mind to gain a greater understanding of God and His workings. The concept is that without the use of the mind there is no Islam. It is that spiritually, all people are equals, because all have the capacity to use their reason. In fact, it warns against acting in a pompous, self-righteous manner. Instead, its focus is on education, that is the education of the soul, regarding right and wrong or good and evil. It also emphasizes the understanding of the attributes of God. This understanding is critical, since humans are readily misguided. Apparently, God is well aware that humans tend to descend into intellectual stagnation. He is aware of the danger of illiteracy or, in fact, as is seen in many parts of North America today, impaired literacy. Here, the focus is on achieving a deep understanding of the nature of God. This is where great misunderstandings occur. People attempt to serve a God they fail to understand. If they could only understand His true nature, they could serve Him more resolutely. In other words, people may think they understand God, but may, unknowingly, be basing this on ignorance.

The word "read" was instituted for a specific impact. This concept was the only one presented to the Prophet Muhammad for a period of three years. Why three years with no other revelation? Perhaps it was to establish clearly the nature of true worship, that is to understand that rather than canonical or dogmatic religion the objective is to use the mind to gain a greater understanding of God. It is to achieve a clear understanding of the human role before Him. That is a far more accurate definition of Islam than mere religious membership. What's more, if worship was the most critical factor, God would have begun the

Qur'an with it, that is instead of "Read" He would have begun with "Worship." The fact is the latter would have been a catastrophe: Islam would have never developed. Nor would have modern science or civilization. This is why He chose a diametrically opposed concept. "Worship" implies rote submission. To some degree it implies seclusion or self-denial. In other words, no thinking is required. All that is needed is to perform the rituals, which even an illiterate person can do. True, worship is a physical/spiritual obligation. However, "Read" is an entirely different matter. Its implications are profound. It is that learning is worship, rather, the essence of it. There can be no other interpretation. It is, apparently, almighty God's perspective.

Worship and Scientific Study: Divine Duties?

People often resist new ideas. It takes work, rather, bravery, to truly accept new ideas. To maintain an open mind is rare. However, by keeping an open mind the opportunity for growth is dramatically increased. With a closed mind there is no growth. Islam is about effort. It is about change. It is about accepting new ideas. It is about self-improvement. It is about advancing the self through a deeper understanding of God. Plus, it is about tolerance.

Islam means submission of human desires for the desires of almighty God. When it began, it was meant to be a movement. This is its purpose today. It is meant to create change at the deepest level possible. The act of submission implies both commitment and concerted effort. This is because submission is similar in meaning to the word, "slave." A poor effort implies a poor 'Islam', that is derelict submission. Mere worship alone is insufficient. An effort must be made to understand the principles of faith, otherwise, religion becomes mere formalities. The fact is the practice of mere ritual alone can never sustain a religious movement. Such a movement can only result from the deepest commitment. It is a commitment based upon a profound understanding. It is the understanding necessary to take action against evil and tyrannical forces. Without change, there is no Islam: period.

Many religious people might argue this point. This is precisely the issue, that is such individuals may well be "religious," while possibly lacking the knowledge or understanding of what true religion or belief implies. What's more, Islam was never meant as a religion. The fact is it is a definition, which is the utter and absolute submission of the self to God. This is its true purpose. To submit would imply to enslave the self, that is to constrain the desires of self-interest for a higher purpose: the desires of almighty God. Unless the definition is adhered to Islam fails to exist. Thus, the outward appearance of Islam, that is mosques, minaret, "Islamic" dress, prayer gatherings, etc., is of little consequence compared to a true commitment. The fact is to be a "Muslim" is by definition to be a slave (or servant) of God. Outward appearance is insignificant. It will offer little if any substance in the final outcome. Rather, it is what is in the heart that is paramount. If this key issue is lacking, that is this spirit of submission, there is no Islam. By this definition any effort less than enslavement implies being a Muslim only by name. What's more, to follow Islam as a "religion" is, in fact, a deviation. Certainly, it is a deviation from the type practiced by Prophet Muhammad. This is because it is what the individual truly becomes as a living example that is defined as Islam, not mere religious association. Yet, who else is there to serve: mere human powers? Islam asks the individual, as well as society in general, to alter the status quo, that is from the servitude of humans to other humans to the service of humans to God. Thus, Islam, is also a force: the force for change.

According to this concept Paradise is available only to those who submit. What's more, there are levels of paradise based upon the degree of submission. This is why it is crucial to understand the true definition of Islam.

The concept of being a slave implies hard work. In other words, an individual's Islam is dependent upon the effort, not mere heredity or formal practice. To seek and gain knowledge is never easy. For instance, to gain a professional degree requires enormous effort, far more than most people are willing to expend, certainly far more than the mere practicing of religious rituals. True, the rituals are essential, in fact, mandatory. Such practices also require a concerted effort and must be performed resolutely. For instance, in Islam ritual prayer and fasting are mandatory. These practices greatly improve both spiritual and physical health. Yet, while these practices serve critical purposes, they are of minor importance compared to the seeking of knowledge. The point is it is insufficient to adhere exclusively to rituals, while neglecting the pursuit of learning. The fact is without the improvement or gaining of knowledge the practice of ritual, while required, is largely futile. This is because ignorance is the opposite of true worship, since knowledge is required to truly understand the nature and power of God. It is also because ignorance is highly dangerous. Ultimately, it is because ignorance leads to the destruction of civilization. God is in no need of mere formalities. Rather, He requires human commitment. In fact, He is in demand of the power offered by the fullest submission of souls.

Again, people might argue this point. Yet, it is indisputable. The Prophet Muhammad demonstrated his true position regarding this. When entering a worship center, he noticed two groups, one pursuing devout worship and the other engaged in active discussion. As a demonstration of his regard for the critical importance of seeking knowledge instead of attaching himself to the faithful devotees he purposely joined the discussion group. This proves that this unlettered man regarded rote spirituality as inferior to intellectual advancement. He knew that mere formality, that is mere ritual prayer, worship, and fasting without deeper commitment was valueless. In other words, he knew that it would fail to produce physical, that is measurable, results. He realized that merely following such practices would fail to achieve the true purpose of Islam: social regeneration. The fact is he realized that only through mental advancements—the advancements that result from intellectual growth—could civilization progress. This explains why his emphasis on education was even more pronounced than on religious rites. Today's world illustrates the inferiority of ritual to deep study. Everywhere, Muslims pray and fast. Yet, they are materially the weakest of all peoples. As a civilization they remain largely illiterate, essentially never advancing their minds. In contrast, the literacy rates in Christian populations are exceptionally high. In Jewish populations they are even higher. This confirms the brilliance of the Prophet's position, that is that it is a sacred obligation to become educated. Without a thorough education there is little if any value to religion.Yet, incredibly, his advice for education was not primarily in religious studies. Rather, it was in the study of the material world. By far, rather than being an ascetic Muhammad was materialistically inclined. More correctly, he was a practical man. He involved himself in all aspects of the material world. True, he was devout, but never to an excess. If his emphasis were on spirituality or mere religious learning, surely, in the aforementioned example he would have joined the prayer group. What's more, if his prerogative were sainthood, he would have emphasized clerical learning. In fact, he stressed the opposite, because it was this man alone who stimulated all civilization to discover, investigate, and upgrade material knowledge from all over the world. He knew that it is the experiences of life, that is the active and persistent involvement in it, that create wisdom, not mere formalities. Regarding the learning process the Prophet was uninhibited. He never condemned the learning of other civilizations as wrong or pagan. Knowledge was to be valued, whether it was produced by a God-fearing society or an atheistic one. In fact, he urged his followers rather, commanded them, to seek knowledge from all people. It was this man alone who made it obligatory for his followers to traverse the earth in search of learning, whether to China, Greece, Rome, Hindustan, Europe or anywhere else. No other ruler enforced such a policy. The type of knowledge produced by these societies, whether divine or polytheistic, was never the issue. The issue was open discovery for the sake of human advancement. Thus, his adherents travelled great distances at any cost and effort to discover and advance knowledge, even if it meant risking their lives. The scholars of Islam regarded it as a divine obligation to advance knowledge. Moreover, certain scholars claim that ignorance of the material sciences is tantamount to disbelief, the latter being a crime in Islam.

Regarding the importance of education the Prophet's followers took his commandments seriously. Thus, it is no surprise that according to Thomas Goldstein, Robert Briffault, and George Sarton it was Islam, not Christianity, which created the material sciences. Furthermore, hindering the advancement of science, that

184 Science and Religion

is legitimate science, the type which advances the cause of humanity without detracting from it, is its very antithesis. By freeing the world's peoples of their inherent biases, Prophet Muhammad revolutionized civilization, creating the basis for the most refined and educated civilization ever to exist. Incredibly, the exact sciences, which are so greatly admired in this secular world, were far from secular. Rather, they were produced by God-fearing people, not atheistic ones. They were produced by those who submit, i.e. Muslims. To a lesser degree they were produced by Jews and, particularly, Christians, who lived under the environment of submission, i.e. who lived under the authority of Islam. They were produced as a consequence of the dictates of the Prophet Muhammad, who sought to elevate humanity exclusively in the name of God.

Here, it is important to note the difference between the meaning of Islam and "religion." Again, Islam means submission to God. Thus, in its view whatever God wills is what should be pursued: without question.

For many people it is seemingly convenient to separate the secular from the religious. Religious obligations are kept separate, usually to be performed once per week. Others make religion a priority but relegate it to a scholarly study, while neglecting or avoiding the pursuit of the practical sciences. Yet, incredibly, the definition of Islam is to submit to God alone. The fact is this is His true 'religion.' What does it mean to submit? It means to strive to serve him in every way. As described by S. H.

Pasha it is to strive in order to become the best at any pursuit. If that means being an expert in the sciences, a successful business person, and/or a religious scholar, so be it. If it demands expending many years of effort to achieve a degree to become a specialist in a given field, that is, in fact, an ideal means of serving Him. If it implies gaining significant knowledge about matters of faith, that is also ideal. If it implies working hard at whatever job God has given a person, that is also a great feat. If it means making a thorough study of the Qur'an with the purpose of adopting its principles, that too is a stupendous achievement. Yet, Islam is far from a religion based upon preaching. Nor is it the means to become a "religious scholar." Rather, it is based upon practice. In other words, the necessary ingredient is to live it. This is how it creates its greatest results. Thus, the Qur'an is not meant primarily to be "preached." Rather, it is meant to be lived. In fact, its only true power is in fully practicing it, incorporating it within the deepest recesses of the soul. It is to be incorporated into every aspect of the individual's life, to be molded within the individual to create a superior personality and, therefore, a superior civilization. Its purpose is to remind all people of the powers and glory of almighty God. Plus, its objective is to remind humans that they are utterly responsible for their actions and that, ultimately, they will return to him.

The Qur'an asks its adherents to fight tyranny and oppression in every way possible. It desires the creation of a type of heaven on earth existence, where people live in peace and where they exist in the proper balance. To deliberately violate, that is to harm, the people or creatures of this earth or the earth itself violates its very essence.

Islam seeks the establishment of human decency at any cost, even the cost of the believer's life. This degree of dedication can only be accomplished by the committed believer, who utterly believes in this mission. It is the mission to become of the Qur'an, in spirit and personality. It is to become an example of its profound principles. It is to act as God's representative on earth. It is to do so in order to make this earth a superior place to live. It is a serious mission, which is to dedicate the self to the struggle against tyranny, oppression, and corruption. It is the struggle to elevate the self against the temptation of a care-free life: the mundane, the apathetic, and the indifferent. It is the struggle to love God and His mission more than one's own self. Islam demands that the individual dedicate his life to the Lord of the Universe. This means that the person must take his or her role in life seriously. It is also the opposite of the self-centered way that most people live today. Furthermore, the Qur'an requires that the individual make a definite commitment, while warning against a half-hearted effort. This is because such a commitment will be tested. An indifferent attitude will readily become evident. Thus, it is what the individual becomes truly in his heart that is the most crucial. It is his deeds and actions that are the true barometers, not what he says. In Islam talk is insignificant. The real determinant is an individual's actions. This was the attitude of the original Muslims. This is why they created the most glorious civilization ever known. Thus, people who preach the principles of the Qur'an today should be in a sense evaluated: does the person truly practice what he preaches? If not, why should such a person be listened to? If the Qur'an is truly a divine book, what else is there to follow? If it is the most contemporary divine book, is there any other to adhere to? If it is the last and most recent revelation, wouldn't it be superior for human guidance than any other? In other words, if it is the most current, accurate, and unaltered text available, is there anything else to rely on? Great consideration should be given to this, because, certainly, humans are in need of guidance. For instance, no one knows what will happen to him after death. What's more, for those who believe in God the question is what is required in order to prepare for the ultimate destiny: the meeting with Him in the afterlife.

Typically, humans make significant efforts to prepare for events in this worldly life, for instance, dinners, picnics, sports outings, vacations, or business meetings. What about the ultimate event, i.e. the meeting with the Creator? It is undeniable that everyone has one issue in common: death. Whether believer or disbeliever, all meet the same fate. The issue is if a person believes in God, as well as in the ultimate meeting with Him, there must be some means of systematically preparing for it. The information for such a preparation is found in the Qur'an. It is found in the form of principles, as well as rules and regulations, regarding how to live in the most ideal state, both for this life as well as the afterlife. Thus, if properly understood, the Qur'an is a treasure trove for personal development. It is self explanatory. Here, the person may study the rules of God on his own. Yet, it may be necessary to find an individual who truly practices it in order to fully understand it. It has a specific history, which is helpful to understand. This is why those who are familiar with it can greatly facilitate its study. However, to learn from a mere "preacher" is insufficient. Rather, it is necessary to find someone who truly lives it. For more details on the study of the Qur'an see the Appendix.

Irrefutable Evidence

While the Qur'an is rich in undeniable truths, such as the rotational nature of the earth, the reflection off the moon of solar light, the gaseous nature of the original universe, the watery origins of life, the origins of life from mineral muck, the action of wind in pollination, the origin of the universe through a cosmic explosion, and much more, the purpose of such truths is primarily spiritual. In other words, these messages are an attempt to reach peoples' hearts by causing them to recognize the existence of God, rather, the role He plays in their very lives. What's more, they are an attempt to cause people to feel grateful for God's blessings, strictly for their own sakes.

The Qur'an's validity, as well as the existence of God Himself, is far from dependent upon the evidences of modern science. Clearly, the Qur'an claims to be the truth itself. It states that its words are incontestable. It claims that none of its concepts can be disproved. No other book makes such claims. In contrast, the Bible contains sections which are known to be falsified. What's more, much of it was written decades, even centuries, after its revelation. Yet, this is no attempt to prove the superiority of one system versus another, one religion in preference to another. Indeed, the Qur'an is opposed to causing arguments regarding matters of belief. If such arguments ensue, the "believer" is commanded to avoid the discussion. Rather, the concept is that those who truly submit, i.e. Muslims (from the Arabic word to submit), must rely on Him alone as their source of inspiration. Thus, they are free of any need to rely upon human beings for the ultimate truths. As described by S. H. Pasha the ultimate evidence and complete reassurance comes from the Qur'an itself through its opening statement: "This is the Book of God, there is no doubt about it." No other book has ever made this claim. Of the millions of books written throughout history, religious, scientific, or historical, no other opens with the statement that whatever it contains, "there is no doubt about it." While the Qur'an professes here to be the ultimate truth, science claims to be devoid of it. This, then, is a self confession from both the Qur'an and science, one of truth versus non-truth, one of ultimate reality versus theory, conjecture, and speculation.

There are a number of statements in the Qur'an which hint at the origins of the universe. For instance, it proclaims that, originally, the universe, apparently after the Big Bang, consisted of a type of smoky material. Science today describes this as stellar dust. The Qur'an indicates that this dust ultimately became the various heavenly objects now in existence. This is precisely the modern finding. For instance, Robert Jastrow in his book, *God and the Astronomers,* confirms the Qur'anic claim, stating that the early universe was a "thick fog" of radiation. Moreover, the Qur'an continues with: "...it is We who have constructed the universe through (an internal) power, and it is We who are steadily expanding it." This is an incredible statement, that is that there is a constant power source, essentially, an infinitely powerful and ever-lasting generator, which drives the expansion of the universe. In other words, the universe is an active system, not a stable or uniform one. This is confirmed by the latest scientific evidence, that is that the universe, far from being static, is constantly changing and growing. The fact that the universe is expanding has been clearly determined by modern astronomers. According to George Smoot, in his book, *Wrinkles in Time*, the discovery that the universe is expanding represented "a vital moment in the development of modern cosmology (the latter term means the study of the universe)." Yet, this "discovery" was only made in the 1920s. What's more, as is confirmed by Smoot it is known with certainty that stellar dust is the raw material for the formation of new stars. Over 1400 years ago both of these modern discoveries were categorically described in the Qur'an. In addition, scientists have proven that new activity is constantly happening throughout the universe. New stars and planets are being formed on a daily basis: before astronomers very eyes. Such an active universe is fully a 2003 discovery. Yet, it is a discovery made originally by the Qur'an, some 1400 years ago. Additionally, the mention previously of the existence of an "internal power," which drives the universe, disputes the commonly held thinking that there is no active power source. This, then, is a refutation from the Qur'an regarding the human claim that an active God is lacking. Rather, it categorically states that the very existence of the universe is dependent upon His vast powers, both originally and now.

Still, there are those who would believe that the Qur'an is man-made, perhaps written by the Prophet Muhammad. True, it originated in the seventh century A.D. True, he represented it. Yet, regarding a moving and expanding universe it would have been impossible for anyone living in that era to conceive of such findings. Even those schooled in ancient astronomy would be unaware of this, since the reigning thought, that of Ptolemy, kept the earth at the center of the universe, with the universe being finite. The stars were thought to be fixed to an invisible background. These ideas of

Ptolemy were known only to a few monks, who guard-
ed ancient manuscripts. Yet, the fact is if they were
available to Muhammad and if he were truly the
Qur'an's author, surely he would have represented these
erroneous ideas. Rather, the Qur'an is free from such
astronomical blunders. Rather, it speaks of concepts
unknown until the 20th century. Therefore, humans
played no role in its creation. In antiquity the best
humans could conceive, that is the works of the ancient
Greeks, were riddled with errors. In contrast, the astronomical statements in the Qur'an are indisputable.

As late as the 1930s the idea of the nature of the universe was in dispute. There was a constant battle
between astronomers regarding whether the universe
was static or perhaps of a different nature. Then,
because of the works of Edwin Hubble, after whom the
famous Hubble Telescope is named, it was confirmed
that the universe is not only infinite: it is also enlarging.
Einstein himself maintained that it was static, in other
words, it never expands. The Qur'an says it is constantly expanding. Thus, the latter is certainly more
advanced in its views than the views of the world-
famous Einstein, who vigorously resisted the idea of a
growing universe. Einstein was wrong; the Qur'an is
right. This seventh century document represents what
Einstein failed to comprehend and what Hubble
tediously discovered. Thus, obviously, these are not the
words of any human or prophet. They must have arisen
from another source. That source is logically almighty

God. Yet, incredibly, Einstein refuted another Qur'anic concept, that is the Big Bang. Smoot says he regarded this theory as "absurd." Yet, the Qur'an confirms its occurrence. Modern science also confirms it. A new satellite has measured data that according to *The Astrophysics Journal* confirms the Big Bang "in detail." This satellite found definitive evidence of background radiation from the original explosion, even finding ancient explosion-related fires. This again demonstrates the ultimate source of this document. After all, in the seventh century it was the Qur'an alone which claimed that all life began as stellar dust and also that, despite what appears to be a stable universe around us, rather, the universe is rapidly expanding, essentially at the speed of light. This is precisely the 21st century finding. Again, it was the internationally renowned astrophysicist George Smoot who claimed that the universe is definitely expanding and that humankind "has emerged from the dust of stars..." Both of these concepts are elucidated in the Qur'an. Thus, who else could be its source, that is other than almighty God?

While during ancient times the moon was known to be a heavenly body, the source of its light was unknown. Yet, the Qur'an proclaims, "He it is Who has made...the moon a (source of) reflective light." Serious thought should be given regarding the origin of such a statement: human or divine? The fact is it behooves the individual to consider it as divine. This is because if such a document is truly from God, what a travesty it would be to ignore or refute it without at least a thorough investigation. What's more, from what other source could it have originated?

The idea that it was written by Muhammad or any of his associates is readily debunked. This man was utterly illiterate and had never written so much as a sentence prior. The fact is he was unable to sign even his name. He had no access to schools or scholars. There were no schools in ancient Mecca. Some have claimed he derived the Qur'an from previous scriptures, yet his interaction with Christians or Jews was virtually nil. Thus, any similarities with these scriptures are not from him. Rather, they are from the same source which originated the previous scriptures. Furthermore, the Qur'an is a vast text, containing 114 sections. It propounds historical data, that is in relation to assisting a person's spiritual growth, principles of faith, rules of divine responsibility, astronomical/biological facts, descriptions of the unknown, regulations for proper business conduct, rules for law and order, dietary prohibitions, rules for women's rights, rules for inheritance, and similar social regulations. The rules and regulations alone defy a human source. Each has a specific social value. Each has been used by humans for over 1400 years. What's more, upon analysis each has such value that it could be the subject of an entire book. These rules have never been altered. In contrast, consider human laws, for instance, the Constitution of the United States. Such laws undergo constant alteration, known as amendments. In contrast, the laws of

Muhammad have never been amended, because the fact is they are immutable. If they were his laws—if they were man-made—certainly, they would have been revised. The Qur'an addresses every aspect of human behavior. Within it are recommendations for an entire social structure. It would take teams of men, rather, entire legions, to even begin such a project let alone complete it in a short 23 years, i.e. the length of Muhammad's mission. Furthermore, many of its statements would only be known to historical or scientific scholars. There were no such scholars in existence at the time of the Qur'an's revelation, that is sixth/seventh century Arabia. Nor were there any scholars of equivalent repute in the surrounding regions. What's more, as mentioned previously, there were no schools or universities where an individual could learn such scientific facts. Yet, even if there were such institutions and even if this man were thereby tutored, of what consequence would it be? Qur'anic statements, such as the existence of a watery origin of life, the origin of existence from stellar dust, and the idea of an expanding (versus static) universe: these are exclusively 20th century discoveries. What's more, the concept of the primal, molecular basis of existence is exclusively modern. No one in the seventh century had any concept about hydrogen atoms. Thus, regarding the Qur'an is there any other conclusion other than it must be from almighty God? Who is it that wrote about 20th century findings such as the origin and purpose of stellar gas and intergalactic dust, the reflective power of solar rays as well as the watery origin of life? It could only be God, not any man.

In contrast to other scriptures the tone of the Qur'an is devoid of special interests. Rather, it speaks directly to humankind. In fact, the attachment to a specific group, like a club, organization, culture, or race, is its antithesis. Its only "groups" are those associated with God. Its only members are those who love and worship Him. This is the only "club" of Islam. To gather people on any other basis, such as race, language, or culture, is its antithesis. This is a major, in fact, catastrophic error. The fact is according to the prophet himself anyone who does so—anyone who holds a certain race or group as elite—is out of its fold. In other words, they cannot be Muslim. In Islam people are all the same: All must ultimately submit. All must return to God. All will eventually be on an equal footing. Thus, the Qur'an is a universal document with a universal message. Anyone can study it, and anyone can become an expert in it. The fact is its true value is far from merely becoming a Qur'anic authority or mere memorization. It is in practicing it. It is in thoroughly understanding it, while acting upon it. This clearly illustrates why the Qur'an is so universal: whoever practices it the most thoroughly and sincerely —whoever understands it the most purely—becomes its greatest scholar, that is its greatest example. This means that regardless of a person's background anyone can become its disciple. Thus, only when an individual lives the Qur'an is he truly a believer in it.

From the Qur'anic point of view knowledge is universal: everyone should have access to it. What's more, withholding or corrupting it is a crime. This is because a lack of knowledge leads to repression, both for the individual and society as a whole. If the mind itself is the victim of repression, that is if due to a lack of knowledge or perhaps misconstrued information an individual's self image is distorted, the entire society is affected. The derogatory effects of misinformation are impossible to quantify. The entire course of history may be altered. Thus, regarding any issue, because of the harm it creates, withholding or repressing the truth is criminal. Regarding the Qur'an it belongs to no special group. Rather, it is a document for all regardless of race, social status, or religion. The fact is it speaks directly to humankind. The Qur'an itself speaks with "you people," "you humankind," or "you human race" while never, for instance, "you Muslims." Thus, all people have the same opportunity to become its scholar.

From the Qur'anic point of view all humans are equal. Thus, its message is the antithesis of the priesthood or elite. Self-denial through becoming a priest, monk, or nun is regarded as a man-made element. Furthermore, there is no requirement of a human intermediary. What's more, to lord over others or to act in a self-righteous manner is regarded as a crime.

This absolute equality of all people is categorically elucidated by the Qur'an (section 14). Here, it describes life after death, claiming that at that time "everyone will appear (as equals) before God." In other words, even those who on this earth arrogantly ruled over others or held themselves superior will eventually be on the same level as all others, that is in the Court of God. Regarding what is clearly an indication of the utter equality of the human race the Qur'an claims that during judgement "...all will be judged, so that God can compensate every human being for whatever he has earned."

Thus, the Qur'an presents a message, which is exclusively for the benefit of the human race. In contrast to other divine texts, no group is given special treatment. Its objective is to warn humans—all of them—for their own benefit. Its purpose is to cause human beings to consider the blessings given to them by their Lord. It is also to cause them to consider their responsibility to Him as their creator. Its aim is to inform them that without exception they will return to Him. Then, all people will be held equal, with the only distinguishing factor being the level of belief and good works.

The Qur'an is far from a document describing mere hell and damnation. It is never meant as a tool to judge people. Rather, it requests that humans only love each other. The fact is, incredibly, in its nearly 100 pages this is its only worldly demand. Regarding people of other cultures, races, or religions being hostile to them or judgmental is discouraged. In this respect it describes God as the only judge. In other words, besides Him no one has the right to judge. What will happen to each individual is strictly His decision: God asks humans to leave judgement to Him. He will determine what will happen to each person. The Qur'an represents primarily a type of warning. Specifically, it is a warning for the prevention of human harm. Thus, it describes what is helpful and harmful, useful and destructive, good and evil. Yet, it also illustrates how the human race can protect itself from self doom. Another claim exclusive to the Qur'an is that every living being is dependent upon God for its survival/sustenance. Furthermore, regarding all creatures it proclaims that God is so incredibly thorough, as well as loving, that He, in fact, knows where everything in existence resides and, ultimately, where and when it will die. Regarding such creatures it says, essentially, "He knows where it lives and where it will die." This illustrates a profound concept, that is that without exception every creature in existence, large or small, monumental or microscopic, is under the management, as well as evaluation, of almighty God. Everything in existence is dependent upon His infinite blessings. Every living being is responsible to Him. In what is an incredible feat, simultaneously, He oversees and cares for all that exists. He assists, monitors, and manages all creatures: solely. In other words, He keeps watch on every being in existence, while also providing for it. Thus, according to the Qur'an nothing escapes His care and review. In fact, He manages it all in excruciating detail. In particular, in regards to humans He is, apparently, dissatisfied with mediocrity. Thus, all humans are constantly under His watch, rule, and critique. True, God loves human beings. Certainly, above all He is forgiving and merciful. Yet, He demands that they act as His representatives. This is a weighty responsibility. Yet, it is a responsibility, which, if properly fulfilled, results in enormous rewards.

Thus, from the Islamic point of view human beings have been created with an elegant essence—a high position. This is the position known as the representative of God. It is up to the individual to pursue such a position, that is to actively seek His pleasure. The Qur'an describes the benefits of such an undertaking as unimaginably great. According to it for those who are truly dedicated to Him there is unlimited success, plus the stupendous news of "happiness in all lives, this as well as the next life." This is an enormous reward, one that any reasonable, that is rational, person must consider pursuing.

Only those who dedicate themselves will achieve the ultimate heights. Yet, what else is there to pursue? The fact that God selected human beings alone as His representatives fully illustrates the importance of such a position.

To represent God is a stupendous thing. The Qur'an describes the benefits of such an undertaking as unimaginably great. Here, it claims that for those who truly dedicated themselves to Him there is unlimited success. Plus, again, there is the stupendous news of "happiness in both lives, this and the next."

True, God is merciful. He never expects more from a person beyond his or her capacity. Yet, His mercy is beyond measure. Thus, for minor achievements He might grant the most unexpected reward. To feed a hungry soul, to help a sick person, to aid a hungry or wounded animal, all are regarded as tremendous achievements. To say even a kind word: this is an immense deed. Such basic accomplishments could earn the individual infinite rewards in the next life.

Human existence is for a definite purpose. Thus, in His view the creation of human life is of a great significance. God made the effort to create each unique being. No one should allow his or her life to be wasted. There is a special aspect to each human, a particular dignity. Life is meant as a serious endeavor. Thus, Islam's view is that a human life, which is wasted, is an immeasurable loss. This is why the idea of working for God is so important. Such a dedication maximizes an individual's potential in preparation for the ultimate result: life after death. The Qur'an makes its position obvious. It is that the doing of good for God's sake leads to greater good, both here and in the hereafter. In contrast, the doing of evil creates greater evil as well as ultimate doom.

Ultimately, everyone will die. The question is what is being done to prepare for what will be from the Qur'anic point of view a far more significant existence, that is the permanence of the afterlife. So indicates the Qur'an in section ten, when it says, "It is God alone who originally creates and, then, recreates." This is the Qur'anic point of view regarding life after death. Here, God has the almighty power to regenerate the dead. Yet, in its own practical way the Qur'an describes that for many people this is incomprehensible. Thus, it states that despite the fact that God has full power over humans and despite the use of reasonable arguments to cause people to think, "they will not believe." Regarding humankind in the Qur'an's simplistic point of view regardless of the arguments presented "some eventually will believe and some will never believe." This raises an interesting argument. If it was truly from other than God, would such a realistic view be taken? If it were man-made, surely the author would never in advance proclaim failure. Surely, he would proclaim instead success. People are notoriously self-serving. Wouldn't a human document seek a more patronizing approach? The Qur'an describes how people react to it in advance: even negatively. No human document could perform such a feat.

Regarding the aforementioned issue of God as a constant creator, i.e. that He "creates and recreates," there is yet another meaning. It relates to evolution. This statement matches the actual fossil record. It does so more accurately than any Darwinian theory. In analyzing changes in the fossil record G. R. Taylor describes dozens of examples of the sudden creation of new species: without any evidence of gradual or unguided evolution. He quotes Ernst Mayr, an avowed evolutionist, who claimed that in the evolution of animals a system is followed. In fact, according to Mayr the fossil record proves that such evolution is "decisively directed...as if *someone* had directed the course (italics mine)."

Therefore, the Qur'anic dictum that "God creates and recreates" is the only plausible explanation for the existing fossil record, that is that, suddenly, species existed and even more suddenly they disappeared, only to be abruptly and unexpectedly replaced by another unique species. How else could this occur other than through the intervention of a divine coordinator? Darwin claims that evolution, i.e. the alteration of the species for survival, occurs only gradually. In his theory sudden changes would be impossible. Thus, evolution offers no explanation for the actual fossil record. Taylor, who is the author of the *Great Evolution Mystery*, further claims that evolution occurs through a detailed plan. He even states that such a plan demands the existence of an *active force*. He further states that in the creation of new species advance thinking was required. Thus, what other option is there, that is who else could be the source of a carefully thought out plan, other than God almighty Himself?

Regarding the human race God makes no distinctions. In other words, He has no favorites. No one is given special credit. Nor does He favor any specific religious group. This scheme of universal equality is demonstrated by the Qur'an itself with: "Rest assured that whoever from among the Muslims, the Jews, the Christians, or any other monotheistic believers, (i.e. literally, 'Sabaeen'), who believe in God and resurrection and perform good deeds he will have his reward with His Lord and has no reason to fear."

In God's world the only special status is through effort. According to Islam the way to achieve such a status is through serving God in every possible way. Thus, in God's realm status is independent of any worldly circumstances such as income level, social position, or race. The fact is whoever serves Him the most intensely and works on His behalf the most brilliantly, whoever strives for His cause the most sincerely and lovingly, that is the status distinction in Islam. Thus, it is only the sincerity of the faith along with the level and amount of good deeds which gives an individual a distinguished position before God.

Finally, the universal, unrestricted tone of the Qur'an is readily described by, "This is the revelation of a book in which there is no doubt, the clear truth from the Lord of the *worlds* (italics mine)." Through this statement the Qur'an confirms what modern science has only recently accepted: that is in this vast universe there is other life. Certainly, it is now believed that there are thousands, perhaps millions, of earth-like planets. If they are earth-like, they must sustain life. For the Qur'an this is elementary knowledge. The fact is in at least two of its sections it confirms the unfathomable: that there truly are other earths. For instance, in section 65 the Qur'an claims, "God is the One who created numerous celestial systems, each with (its own) earths." This serves as a proof from almighty God regarding His immeasurable greatness. It is a means of perhaps humbling the human race, that is to realize that it is far from unique. This concept is completed in section 42 with, "One of His proofs is the creation of the heavens and the earth(s), plus the various living beings he has scattered (throughout them)." Thus, the Qur'an is adamant: non-earthly life forms exist, apparently in a wide, perhaps infinite, variety.

Because of the vastness of the universe, mathematically, the probability of earth-like planets is high. Astronomers are now convinced that throughout the universe earth-like planets exist. This was described in the Qur'an hundreds of years ago. However, it is only the Qur'an which indicates the true vastness of the living universe, indicating that, essentially, there are thousands, even millions, of earths, each teeming with life.

Today, the possibility of life on other planets is fully confirmed. This is because water has been found on at least one other planet: Mars. Therefore, life must exist there, at least the microbial type, though scientists are hesitant to admit it. What's more, there are thousands of other planets in this universe, perhaps millions, which contain water. There must be other water-nourished planets. The circumstances for the creation of water and, therefore, life cannot be solely unique to the earth. This is because there are trillions of stars or "suns" and, thus, potentially billions of planets. It is only logical that a plethora of these planets must sustain life. Where there is water, there is also life. This is because the existence of water means that there is oxygen in the atmosphere, and oxygen reveals the presence of life. There is only one way in which oxygen can be continuously produced: from living beings. Thus, regarding the vast unknown universe what the sages of the past propounded appears to be true, which is that there exist multiple worlds, multiple earths, and innumerable forms of life utterly unknown to us.

There is no question that among the many spheres in this universe the Earth is unique. It may be God's finest planet. This is why serious thought should be given to how the Earth is treated. The Islamic view is to avoid harming it at any cost.

Today, scientists agree that life on other planets is a reality. When science as an institution was non-existent, the Qur'an elucidated this very concept, one which it took modern scientists centuries to confirm.

Yet, the earth, despite its uniqueness, has a dire future. It will be destroyed. All life will cease. Every creature will die. Eventually, only lifeless dust will remain. Only God will survive. Thus, is there anyone else to rely upon—is there anyone else to turn to—other than His almighty self? When human life ends, nothing that is accumulated will be of value. Wealth and social power will be inconsequential. The Islamic view is that only good deeds and God are eternal. The destruction of civilization is perhaps closer than many believe. It could occur sooner than imaginable. The fact is it is likely to occur at any moment. This is because the signs evident in all scripture are clear, particularly the decline of morality and the willingness to support the forces of evil.

Evil has overcome good. The trend must be reversed. The refusal to reverse it, that is to combat the evil forces which control human destiny, will result in dire consequences. The fact is the willingness to accept evil trends will rapidly conclude in human extermination. If evil is allowed to proceed uninhibited, it will flourish, ultimately overpowering all good. This will lead to the most dire consequences: global human catastrophe. When such a calamity strikes, there will be no escape. Only belief in God, as well as good acts, can offer protection. This is the only formula for ultimate happiness as well as success. What's more, it is the only means to protect the soul from ultimate doom.

Chapter Six
Conclusion

Rather than a religion Islam is a definition. It means peace. It is the peace which results from the submission of the self to the will of almighty God. It is the peace of forgoing personal desires for the desires, as well as the rules, of the Creator. Such a creator desires for humans to adopt a specific trend: to be decent, honest, upright citizens. He is the same Being who provides rules, and the only beneficiaries are human beings.

Islam is a system which provides such rules. It represents peace, that is the peace of turning over the self, without resistance, to the command and desires of almighty God. It is the serenity, as well as love, that arises from serving God instead of the interests of men. Islam is the means to achieve great heights. It provides all the necessary methods for human advancement. The concept is simple. God created human beings and, therefore, knows what is best for them. This is why the Qur'an contains specific rules for how to live. It is also why it contains certain prohibitions. Its regulations were designed to prevent self-harm. Thus, its rules for behavior, both for human beings individually and societies in general, were created to prevent strife, tyranny, ill health, and misery, that is human harm of any type. The point is simple. God, the creator of human beings, knows what are the latter's true needs. Thus, He knows what is best for them. Yet, its systems serve a single goal: the establishment of the divine rule instead of the rule of men.

Islam must never be represented as easy. Rather, it means self-sacrifice. The term itself means submission. Thus, it is the ultimate sacrifice: the giving of the self to God. It is the sacrifice of abandoning self-interest and pride for the sake of humble service. It is the repressing of carnal desires for the desire of serving His almighty Self. It is the willingness to work hard, not for self-gain but for the gain of the greater good. It is the sacrifice of seeking no reward, that is until the end of time. Yet, the consequences of such sacrifice are profound. These consequences are success in two realms, this life and the next.

Today, regarding what a person should believe there is vast confusion. Religion, at least in its orthodox forms, is often found debilitating. This is because it seemingly represents an inordinate degree of rules and rituals. Plus, the beliefs are often distressing, many of which violate common sense. Some are outright hypocritical. The question is are these from God, or are they man-made? Certainly, no one wants to adopt archaic principles or rituals based on ignorance, that is the inventions of mere men. Educated people often find rules and regulations repressive. Thus, people are uncertain of what direction to assume. The Qur'an provides rules and regulations which assist such a pursuit. Thus, rather than being a "holy" book, it is a book for personal guidance. What's more, it provides concepts that create a security of heart. In other words, it creates a sense of confidence in the unknown. Furthermore, it provides its own unique attribute: guidance on demand. It does so in a format uniquely different than human "guidance" such as the type resulting from personal advisers, counselors, psychiatric evaluations, gurus, or astrologers. The Qur'an is completely unique compared to such dubious sources. This is because it offers guidance directly to the individual without the need for an intermediary. It is guidance dictated by a higher power: the great and almighty God.

Because of what it represented, Islam changed the world. As a consequence of what it eradicated, that is the elimination of a self-centered nature, it monumentally elevated human civilization. What's more, even today it upgrades this world, because it represents the commitment of the self exclusively to God. Thus, initially, it created a type of world never before seen, which was exceptionally sophisticated as well as productive.

Islam readily coexists with modern or positive advancements. In fact, as described in the book, *Science in the Name of God* (Dr. Kasem Khaleel), it created the majority of these advancements. Its objective is simple yet revolutionary. It seeks to improve the individual and, ultimately, all civilization. It does so by purifying the individual's heart, cleansing it of all evil, and purging it of any self-destructive emotions. It does so by making a simple demand: submission of the individual to God. This submission is not for God. Rather,

Science and Religion

it is for the specific person and, ultimately, the entire human race. Thus, its purpose is to create a superior world, one in which there are equal rights and a common decency rule. Its concepts are presented herein, because in contrast to many other religions, it coincides with modern science.

In Islam there is a kind of oneness, which unifies all. God Himself is regarded as the source of all laws, including the various scientific principles by which the universe, as well as this world, operate. Thus, if there is a Law of Gravity, it is His invention. If there are laws for the speed of light and sound, they are His. God has the true access to all knowledge, that is He knows the inner workings behind existence. In contrast, human knowledge is comparatively limited. What's more, He is an involved God. Here, God alone is the ultimate source of knowledge. If a human being becomes inspired, He is the source. Ultimately, He is also the source of all stimulation, which motivates human beings to learn, discover, and invent. Thus, His instructions, that is His "laws," couldn't possibly conflict with the truths found in the sciences. The fact is He made the universal laws upon which the sciences are based.

Belief in God is a personal choice. Regarding Him, no one can force another person to believe. Reason can be used to indicate His existence. However, it is up to the person whether he or she decides to accept Him. Thus, it truly is an individual's free will to decide to believe in a Supreme Being or to deny Him. In contrast, science is not a matter of belief. This is because it is a concept, which can only be defined through experiments. Experimentally, religious beliefs, that is the concept of a creative God, are impossible to study. Science is based upon a single principle, with numerous divisions. The various religions are also based upon principles. However, rather than being provable through experiments, these principles are a matter of belief.

Since, historically, certain religions have had a less than productive history regarding the advancement of the sciences, understandably, many scientists regard them as an impediment. They deem religions as repressive influences, a position which is often justified. What's more, they rarely if ever regard them as contributors. Even today certain beliefs maintained by religious sects violate fundamental universal laws. For instance, the Qur'an makes it clear that this universe and everything within it, including the earth, is ancient, beyond human reckoning. Thus, there is no allowance in Islam for restrictive philosophies based purely on dogma, for instance, the belief that God created the earth literally in six days, that the earth is only a circumscribed period of time old, like 6,000 years, or that He made Adam's mate, Eve, from one of his ribs.

The concept of the rib is likely a parable, indicating that women are similar to men, i.e. of the same substance spiritually. It was to indicate that contrary to many popular views they are not alien to each man but are spiritually and emotionally "companions." What's more, it was to indicate that there should be no conflict between them, only utter cooperation, since they arise from the same source: God almighty. Incredibly, had this view, which is based upon reason, become firmly established, untold agony and repression would have been prevented. Women would be more readily understood as being of the same nature as men, rather than as opposites or even adversaries. Similarities would be cultivated rather than differences. They would be viewed as essentially men's equals, while with different attributes. They would be understood as on the same level, both intellectually and spiritually, rather than as underlings. Interactions with women would be on the basis of their intellectual attributes, that is their mental capacities, rather than their physical ones. This is the Islamic view of the male-female interaction. Incredibly, this was also the view of various prophets, including Muhammad and Jesus Christ.

As the aforementioned indicates a literal interpretation of scripture can lead to misconceptions. Such misconceptions can cause a vast degree of distress and even repression. Incredibly, it is conceivable that an almighty God may reveal a certain concept and humans completely misconstrue it. For instance, when mentioning the earth's creation, the Qur'an, like the Bible, uses the term "day." However, it uses it metaphorically, that is as a reference point. It is input to create a common ground for the people of previous scriptures. Originally, in the Bible it may have also been used metaphorically. However, data concerning this is unavailable. According to the Qur'an a day in God's scheme is beyond comprehension. The Qur'an provides a hint at its vastness. It is easy to do the math: simply multiply the concept of divine time, i.e. "a human day is equal to 50,000 divine days" times the days in a year. Thus, a year on the divine calendar would represent several million human days.

It would appear that human life is utterly short. This implies that the time available is precious. This time should be used for productive purposes, which advance the cause of humanity. This was precisely what Islam accomplished. It did so at a time when humanity was hopelessly mired in paganism. Yet, it continues to do so today in the form of individuals who dedicate their all in the service of their mighty master, the Lord of the universe. People may serve many minor masters. Yet, the benefit of such service is limited to few if any gains in this temporary life. Imagine the gains of serving the master of all—the mighty Lord of the universe. Those benefits are beyond measure.

Islam: The Liberal Religion

In contrast to the bigoted nature of medieval or "religious" cultures Islamic civilization was refreshing. This is because it created scientific advancements, while praising the name of God. Islam broadly opened the doors to learning. It did so by eradicating restrictions. It liberalized the learning process by accepting, without bias, the works of every known civilization. No knowledge was disregarded as "pagan." Rather, it was disregarded only if it was impractical or, perhaps, destructive. The fact is the religious practices of other civilizations, while studied, were regarded as insignificant: it was their learning that mattered. If it was practical, if it was useful in everyday life, Islam adopted it. This was regardless of its origin, pagan or pious. In contrast, Europe remained intolerant to outside information, regarding the writings of other cultures as works of the devil. Thus, Islam freed the human mind from such restrictive thinking by demanding the use of reason instead of blind faith.

Today, in certain Muslim groups, particularly those unfamiliar with the original history of Islam, there is a tendency to regard the accomplishments of the West as the works of the devil. Incredibly, this includes learning in the sciences. Thus, any learning in "pagan" lands might be disregarded or viewed as suspect. Yet, originally, the books of other religions or civilizations did not "frighten" Islam. This is because, since it is based on the use of reason, the writings of other peoples could not "corrupt" it. These writings would merely be scrutinized for their potential value. Islam was secure from within. In other words, in the true Islam, that is the Islam which created civilization, the basis for human interaction was the use of the mind rather than blind faith or religious zeal.

Western historians reveal the high degree of perfection achieved by Islam. Some authors, such as Sarton, Goldstein, Briffault, De Vaux, Renan, and Durant, indicate that it alone created the scientific method. Durant notes that in chemistry Islamic scientists were the first to conduct experiments. In mathematics the editors of

the *Encyclopedia of the History of Arabic Science*
clearly indicate that the scientific method originated
in Islam and that this is particularly the case with
precision mathematics. Even so, in standard education
teachers praise the ancient Greeks as the originators
of the scientific method, without providing firm
evidence. The claim for the Greeks as the liberators
is insufficient, since they failed to create a global,
liberal civilization. The fact is their civilization was
exceptionally self-centered. Thus, access to higher
education was restricted, since it was based upon race
or lineage. Outsiders were regarded as inferior intellectually and were never allowed into the fold. What's
more, the Greeks were primarily contemplators, being
heavily involved in theories, many of which were
vague. Plato complained bitterly about the indiffer-
ence of his people to scientific inquiry, even stating
that much of their math was merely inherited and
reworked from Babylonian and Egyptian originals.
Thus, it is only presumed that the Greeks were the
first experimental scientists and on that basis they are
given full credit. The basis of such misinformation is
racial, i.e. to perpetrate the idea that all of the significant developments originated from European
sources. In other words, it is a means of diminishing
the contributions of other races. It is an attempt to
imply that positive contributions to the growth of civilization came from only one source: The Western
world. Specifically, it is a view that the ancient Greeks
and Western Europeans are the true fathers of modern

science. This is despite the fact that the top Western historians refute it. Yet, regardless of the facts of history the view is maintained, in fact, promoted. Why is such blatant misinformation perpetuated? It is done to maintain repression and control. Everywhere Islam is represented as a hostile force, which, somehow, will hurt humanity. It is to indicate that an atheistic or polytheistic society is responsible for the origin of civilization, not a "religious" or, more correctly, God-fearing one. It is to legitimize a civilization based upon man-made rules, that is rules for controlling and manipulating the masses, versus the rules of the almighty God. It is to justify the repression of a people to steal their inalienable rights as well as their material wealth: oil, gas, minerals, and more. It is a specific agenda meant to create harm, not just to Muslims but to people in general. It is to cause a people to become downtrodden, that is to turn them, psychologically, into "second-class citizens." Therefore, it is to perpetuate evil trends, which serve only the interests of the vested few. All who stand in the way of such corrupt elements place their lives at risk. Yet, the basis for any fear, that is the fear of Islam as a hostile or decadent force, has no basis. Rather, it is secular forces that are to be feared. For instance, because of its irrational nature, the Greek religion and the philosophy it propounded stultified scientific progress. Pierre Martineau, former head of advertising at the *Chicago Tribune*, claims that the Greeks were so irrational in their approach that they "never produced any real science." Robert Briffault confirms this, saying that the Greeks despised tedious experimental science. Thus, according to Briffault, Sarton, Goldstein, and many others, the performance of highly detailed work—the work of precise experiments—originated exclusively in Islam. In fact, this was precisely the work that created the modern sciences. This contribution is perhaps best edified by Arthur Selwyn-Brown, Ph.D., in his book, *The Physician Throughout the Ages*, who said that Arabic/Islamic culture was "...entirely responsible for the revival of learning in Europe." Yet, why not? When the Qur'an arrived, the world was spiritually and intellectually incapacitated. This single book regenerated the world, elevating it to a height never before seen. Through it, learning was stimulated to such a profound level that it led to the creation not only of Islamic civilization but also European civilization. What's more, Russia, fully secular, destroyed civilizations: dozens of them. In contrast, Islam is friendly to humanity. Because of it, people today live in a high level of development. It is directly responsible for the modern way of living. It alone was the true liberator. It alone defeated barbarism for the sake of humankind.

For some individuals the aforementioned may seem astounding, even incomprehensible. It may even be difficult to believe for people who are seemingly closely associated: Muslim people or people from the Middle East. This is because of what has been commonly taught. Rather, it is because of the way people have been programmed. Yet, ultimately, it is because of what is obvious. It is the fact that, materially, the Western world is powerful, educated, and, seemingly, sophisticated. What's more, Western powers are apparently completely opposed to anything "Islamic." They claim that this is because Islam is "backward." Furthermore, they claim that by adopting it people will be forced into the "fourteenth century," even the Dark Ages. Yet, there is perhaps some reason for such fears. The so-called Islamic world is utterly lacking in material achievements. What's more, it is visibly decrepit. People desire the lifestyle of such places as the United States, Canada, England, and Europe, and rightfully so. In contrast, few would prefer to live in Saudi Arabia, Egypt, Libya, Algeria, Morroco, Indonesia, Turkey, Iraq, or similar places. In the West there is the rule of law. In the aforementioned "Muslim" countries tyranny, in fact, corruption, largely reigns. Regarding this tyranny, it is largely instituted by the rulers. They are rulers installed directly by Western powers. Yet, incredibly, as described by Sarton, Durant, and Briffault, Islam was precisely the source for the stimulation, as well as creation, of the aforementioned Western structure. It was exactly the source of civilization ultimately modeled by the West. Thus, the great achievements of the West originated with Islam. Therefore, the claim that the establishment of Islam will cause anarchy is baseless. The fact is a modern understanding of it will only result in the further growth of civilization.

Again, admittedly, for many individuals this may seem rather shocking. This is because, clearly, people have been led to believe that modern civilization owes its origin to the West. How is it possible that all the information which has been taught, all the standard education, could be false? How could seemingly outright lies be told? If so, what would be the reason for such fabrications? Is it ignorance, or is there a specific purpose, that is a deliberate agenda, to falsify data? Briffault claimed that the misrepresentation was purposeful, that is there is malicious intent. G. E. Griffin, in his article, *The Great Deception*, claims that specific organizations exist to manipulate the thinking of Americans. He claims that currently these organizations are highly active. One such group, the Carnegie Fund, has as its goal the manipulation of history to serve specific agendas. Whatever the reason, the issue remains clear. The historical record must be corrected. This is so that people can access the most unbiased data possible. It is so that they can formulate their own views of history, *rather than having them formulated for them.*

It is often said that history is "written" by the conquerors to suit a specific purpose. Yet, there is a certain degree of greed, as well as arrogance, behind historical lies. It is the vileness of lying merely to serve special interests. It is the arrogance of the desire to always be in control. It is the hostility, as well as arrogance, of claiming racial or social superiority. It is the tyranny of keeping people subjugated. Yet, regarding human repression it is primarily the greed and lust for wealth which is the motivater. What's more, it is the audacity placing human desires and personal interests over the rule of almighty God. What's more, it is the thirst for unbridled power at any expense, even the damage, death, and destruction of millions, perhaps billions, of lives. It is the audacity of destroying an entire planet to serve the wants of the few.

Yet, are people truly aware that such vile acts are being perpetrated? Regarding the minds of the people could it be that they have been controlled and manipulated, not for their own benefit, but for the benefit of the few, who seek personal gain, glory, and absolute power at any cost? In other words, is it true that, today, modern humans have been relegated to an existence as mere pawns? According to Griffin this is precisely the case. He quotes the fact that prominent organizations, such as the Rockefeller and Carnegie Foundations, have "pooled their resources" specifically to "control the teaching of history." Certainly, it is an issue worth exploring.

Islam means submission to almighty God. Thus, it is resolutely against any such tyranny, that is the tyranny of forcing people to submit to powers other than Him. Today's brand of greedy science would find an adversary in truly Islamic science. It was the 10th century Islamic scientist al-Farabi, who provided an opposing view, which memorialize the contribution of Islam. He said, "If we are unsure of a matter—(if we cannot be certain of its truth)—it is our obligation to remain silent (brackets mine)." If only Western historians and scientists would adopt this view, what a uniquely different world this would be. The fact is this statement by al-Farabi categorically describes the attitude of Islam. It is an attitude to establish human needs—the needs of the everyday people, the needs of human civilization—above the desires or passions of the self or, in particular, the select few. In other words, if the publication of a falsehood could negatively affect this world, if it could hurt people or interfere with the progressive growth of civilization, it must be prohibited. Therefore, according to the Islamic view before an issue can be presented as true, it must be proven absolutely correct. Otherwise, pronouncing it should be avoided. Such an attitude clearly shows Islam's view of the world scene, that is that tyranny or corruption of any type, including the corruption of unbridled self gain, that is the gain for the self at the expense of the people or this planet, is prohibited.

The Qur'an strictly coincides with rational scientific thinking. It is the only revealed text which thoroughly withstands scientific investigation. This means that nothing within it refutes scientific facts. Thus, it compliments, rather, enhances, scientific progress. If only the philosophies of the Qur'an were adopted, life on this planet would improve dramatically, with less trauma both to the planet and its inhabitants. The fact is it is a practical book. Rather than ethereal concepts which are difficult to comprehend it emphasizes life on this planet. Rather than emphasizing the afterlife its focus is the current one, that is it is a guide regarding how to make this life as productive as possible.

Science is amoral. If it is a 'religion' it has proven to be the most diabolical of all. Scientists rarely if ever consider the moral consequences of their actions. This is because in today's brand of science potential harm to humankind is overridden by vested interests. This has led to disastrous consequences. Unless morality, that is accountability, is reinstituted in the sciences, this earth will rapidly end. It must be reinstituted in its true form, because science originated in a moral environment, that is the environment of Islam, the environment of submission to God. Atheists failed to create the sciences, nor did polytheists, that is the Greeks, who worshiped innumerable Gods. The fact is the sciences were created by monotheists. Even today, they are creating them. Islam as a social power would command scientists to consider the consequences of their actions. This is because it is based upon moral good rather than vested or selfish interests. Yet, such a forceful, rather, moral approach, in fact, facilitates scientific achievement. As a result, it is catapulted from the arena of special interests and biased research to the environment of altruism. Thomas Goldstein claims that all the major sciences were Islamic innovations. The point is during the Islamic Era human benefit was the priority, not the interests of the vested few. In all likelihood unless the immorality in science is curbed this earth will self-destruct.

The Qur'an confirms numerous concepts, which still remain mere theories today. Rather than burdening the mind with insignificant details, it provides a type of guidance, which has obvious value. It is a guidance for regenerating the human soul, which is, seemingly, constantly under siege. It is a guidance which is refreshing both to the mind and heart. It is a message which is uplifting, because it offers a means for humanity to reach a profound goal. It is the goal of freeing the self from being beholden to any power other than God. Ultimately, its goal is to free the human being from the repression of man-made rules. It is to release the soul from the tyranny of repression, torment, and "brain-washing," all of which are imposed to meet specific tyrannical agendas. This is because according to the Qur'an there is only one means through which a person can completely flourish: complete submission to God. All must submit; all are equal. Anything which impedes this is to be resisted, in fact, fought. To accept such tyranny, to bow to the status quo, is tantamount to the acceptance of the lordship of humans over the lordship of the true Lord. In Islam this is a form of disbelief. This makes sense, because according to it the very existence of human beings, that is the ability of humans to function and thrive, is strictly a consequence of the blessings and compassion of almighty God. Thus, the Islamic view is that all that exists arises from Him. Considering this fact, truly, all gratitude is due to God. Part of this gratitude is manifested by the resistance by each believer against the tyranny imposed by humans, a tyranny which leads to the destruction of the human race as well as this planet. The believer who resists, in fact, fights, tyranny is in God's eyes an utter saint. This is the highest level for the believer to achieve. Yet, what other option is there? This is because according to Islam the very purpose for the human being is the full-fledged service of God.

Here, the concept is that the soul itself is a divine creation, in fact, it is God's very essence. He naturally exists within it, unless He is forcibly removed, that is by disbelief, hate, self-pity, rage, vile deeds, or anger. It is a soul which is responsible to Him. It is a soul which essentially owes Him his or her life. Anything inferior to this, such as the service of the self to human lords, is catastrophic. Regarding this responsibility it is crucial to remember the simple origins of the human being: stellar dust, water, a muck-like clay, and, ultimately, the minute and utterly dependent embryo. Thus, the concept is that humans originate from God and are utterly dependent on Him. To rebel against Him, despite having such humble beginnings, would be the greatest of all violations. Regarding this submission—this utter dependency—this has always been so, from the germ cell and embryo to the newborn, rather, from stellar dust itself. It is only when a human develops consciousness, that is the ability to think, does he choose against submission. It is only when he can think and argue that he decides against humility and instead chooses arrogance. In other words, submission is his natural tendency, from the fixed, bowed head of the embryo to the dependence of the child to the unmercifully bowed posture of the elderly—all submit, willingly or unwillingly. Even the shadow submits, flattening itself on the earth out of an obligation to His laws. Yet, will the heart willingly submit? This is the greatest deed a human can achieve, to willingly give God His due, to return to Him His right: the ownership of human souls.

Every individual, that is every living soul, is unique. Each has its own specific needs and characteristics. The Islamic view is that God meets the needs of each of them. Such an almighty power would know best what is each person's potential. Such a Being is constantly connected to each individual, providing guidance and uncountable favors. Such guidance may be accepted or rejected. His favors may be recognized or ignored. This is where the power of choice plays such a crucial role. Only humans can choose to honor, that is respond, to divine communication. As well only they can reject it. The wise person recognizes this, accepts the inspiration, and praises God for His graciousness.

Islam claims that the benefits of serving Him are immense, while the consequences of failing to do so are disastrous. Recent research confirms this. Individuals who find solace in the belief in God are significantly less likely to need psychological care and/or mood-altering drugs than people who are uncommitted. Thus, belief in God creates an immense sense of security, one which is impossible to procure through any other means. It is the peace of mind which results from esteeming God as the highest power, while realizing that humans have no ultimate power. Thus, in terms of the ability to alter or control these destinies humans are powerless. They may be able to stall but they cannot halt the inevitable. This is because all that exists must return to Him. Thus, regardless of how much control humans might attempt to exert, the ultimate authority—the final decision—rests with God alone. He is the one Who must be recognized and feared, not mere humans.

According to the Qur'an God expects human gratitude. Yet, He insists this is for each person's benefit, not for Him. To be grateful is a reasonable choice. It is the natural tendency of the human being. It is the tendency of all nature. For instance, animals are exceedingly grateful to their caretakers. Notice how a cat or dog bows, even submits, to its "master." Yet, do humans willingly submit to theirs? The fact is, often, they refuse to do so. Thus, this is the difference between humans and animals. The Qur'anic concept is humans are tested to evaluate whether they are grateful or ungrateful. Animals know no other way, so there is no need to test them. Only humans have the right to choose, that is to either truly believe in Him or reject Him. What's more, according to the Qur'an only humans are specifically being watched, as well as evaluated, by almighty God.

The Qur'an is far from a religious book. Rather, it is a book meant to create change, both in the individual and civilization. Because of its dependence upon the use of reason, the Qur'an catapulted civilization from the ignorance of paganism to the brilliance of learning and sophistication. It is a worldly book. This is why it created material change. Only it eliminated all barriers, which held humanity in check. Directly, it caused civilization to flourish. Ultimately, it stimulated the revival of Europe. It was the book of choice, which motivated the believers to seek and disseminate knowledge as well as to publish it on a wide scale.

The impact of the Qur'an was significantly different than that of other divine texts. This is because it had a measurable influence upon the advancement of civilization. The Qur'an offers a capacity strictly its own. Of the millions of books written in human history it is the only one adamant about its source. It alone states categorically that it is the book of God, while providing proof   for it. For those who doubt it consider the Qur'anic challenge: to duplicate it or even a portion of it. As of yet this has never been attempted. The Qur'an is unique in another respect. No other text claims to categorically be an unaltered divine book, that is a book which no human has corrupted. As eloquently described by S. H. Pasha it is the Qur'an alone which opens with the statement, "This is the book of God: there is no doubt about it." This itself is a stimulation, that is it stimulates the individual to think. It motivates the individual to consider: is this truly from God? The source itself leaves no room for doubt. With its description of whirling celestial spheres, a spherical, in fact, egg-shaped, as well as mobile, earth, a sun bursting with energy, a moon, which functions as a solar mirror, a universe of endless space, an uncountable number of extra-galactic worlds and earths, mountains driven deep into the earth and rising high for modulating centrifugal forces, the creation of the inner earth in a state of turbulence, the watery origin of life, the systematic creation of the human embryo, the creation of milk as a filtrate of blood: all are proofs. They are proofs for an entire globe of people to whom such proclamations are and were unknown.

Thus, it was exclusively the Qur'an which regenerated the human condition. It did so by causing people to think. Of note, previous scriptures lacked a scientific angle. Thus, in terms of revealed texts only it inspired the creation of scientific inquiry. Yet, incredibly, it also inspired creativity of an incomparable degree in the peoples of all religions, whether Christian, Jew, Muslim, or agnostic.

Even today the accomplishments of the Islamic scholars remain unmatched. Consider this: even in today's age, the Age of Information, can anyone name a single person who has written, for instance, 50 books on the sciences or other valuable fields? During the Islamic era there were hundreds, perhaps thousands, of such scholars. Ibn Sina, who lived in the 11th century, wrote over 250 books. Al-Biruni, who thrived in the 13th century, wrote over 100. Al-Haytham produced over 80. All these scientists were experts in multiple fields. Ibn Sina was an internationally renowned expert in pharmacy, medicine, geology, and physics. His books influenced scientific thinking for fully 500 years, a period over twice as long as the existence of the United States. Thus, the immense productivity resulting from Islam to this day remains unmatched. Plus, it still influences every aspect of modern science. The fact is, today, such diversified scholars, that is scholars who publish in numerous fields, are rare. What's more, the existence of scholars whose works dramatically alter the course of history is even more rare. Yet, where they do exist, Islam is their most likely progenitor. This would have to be so. After all, Islam means the utter submission of the self to almighty God. It is this position that creates success. This is because only Islam elevates the individual from the mere pursuit of personal gain to the complete service of almighty God. This is why even today there exists a plethora of diversified scholars, who are humbly serving humanity through their works in various fields. Since their interests are in serving God, little may be known about them, at least publically. They are scholars, who deny public glory for the ultimate glory of pleasing God. This is the only reward they seek. Yet, their works are prominent and invaluable. Thus, today, Islam continues to produce the vast creativity which helps enhance this world and which results from the unbridled service of the human soul to the will and rule of almighty God.

There is no conflict between belief in God and the recognition or study of the sciences. With its definition of abiding by the will of almighty God, Islam requires their study. Certainly, this is partly in order to understand His greatness. Yet, it is equally for the purpose of advancing material accomplishments.

In contrast to the views of medieval Europe Islam maintained the attitude that scientific discoveries could never disrupt the faith of the true believer. It maintained the philosophy that it is incumbent upon the believer to seek knowledge. Here, the profound findings of science only serve to deepen the believer's commitment. Thus, the more deeply the believer investigates nature the more profoundly he sees evidence of God. The fact that the universe is utterly systematic further deepens his belief in His almighty and continuous role. Ultimately, as the search in the sciences deepens the believer senses Him continuously. In all interactions he perceives His magnificent and mighty presence. Thus, he firmly realizes that whatever occurs is utterly dependent upon Him, even his life and death. Yet, as the believer truly comprehends so is the ultimate return: the resurrection, when all in existence, as well as everyone from the past, will come before the Judge of Judges. The believer realizes that it is only God who will preside over this Court, where He will assess the actions of each person, good or evil, right or wrong. Then, all material goods, as well as all human-like powers, will be utterly useless. Money, even trillions of dollars, will have no impact. Only good actions will prevail.

Like the universe and the earth, science adheres to specific laws. Yet, these laws exist only as a result of the efforts of the Law-Maker. Incredibly, humans see only the result of these laws, that is the visible, organized universe and visible life on earth. People see this only because they have the eyes, that is the actual organs, to visualize it. Without the ability to see, the universe, as well as the earth, would seem like an endless, purposeless void. Yet, someone had to create the actual laws and systems which uphold what we see.

Furthermore, someone had to create the capacity to 'see', that is the concept of vision.

In this life all scientific concepts start with an idea. Humans then transform those ideas into real inventions previously unknown: the telephone, steam engine, and airplane. Yet, what kind of mind created the idea of vision, or for that matter, hearing, taste, and smell? What kind of magnificent creature could synthesize the concept of planets, suns, stars, solar systems, galaxies, and infinitely more? What kind of utterly intelligent being could design with perfection such organs as the human eye and ear or the very fingertips, which sense all? Such a concept, that is the creation of a thing from nothingness, as well as the creation of the exact plans, which are behind all that exists, is difficult for humans to conceive. It would require a mind of infinitely high intellect, as well as organization, to conceive of and then bring into reality such systems. The fact is He would be a systematic Being, always planning His creation. Consider the term "solar system." Truly, the creator of this vast universe is systematic, following his own highly organized plan. Such an all-powerful mind operates in a highly organized way. This would imply that all that exists fits into a specific plan. G. R. Taylor asserts in his book, *The Great Evolution Mystery,* that for certain such a plan exists. While he offers no clue regarding who made it, the fact is only the Mighty Master of the universe could perform such incomprehensible feats. Therefore, God may be regarded as the Greatest of all Inventors, since He created the principles of science before anything existed. In other words, it is He alone who made the laws which govern all that exists. Only He created the molds. Humans are incapable of fathoming the design behind, that is the thinking process that caused the creation of the tiniest living being or even a mere rock. Obviously, it is a Being of mighty powers, fully beyond comprehension. He makes all varieties of beings, from the most infinitesimal, like a virus, to the most massive, like a whale or elephant. He makes the utterly beautiful, like the prettiest bird, as well as the bizarre, like a freakish deep sea creature. He makes it all work so perfectly, whether the function of the lowly gnat or the structure of the mathematically perfect molecule. Who else other than God could be responsible? What's more, since He created all that exists, that is the heavenly bodies, so methodically studied in astronomy, this earth, so curiously examined in geology, the atoms, so precisely studied in physics, the biological molecules, so thoroughly analyzed in biochemistry, and the various plants and animals, so deliberately investigated in biology, the study of the sciences may be regarded as the study of God.

Even a casual study of nature is revealing. Every substance or creature demonstrates His presence. The feathers of a duck, which protect it from water, its specialized web feet, which allow it to virtually walk or glide on water, the stealth-like body shape and powerful muscles of a mighty lion, which assist it in capturing and pouncing on its prey, the phenomenally efficient digestive tract of a cow, which is capable of digesting mere grass and turning it into vitamin-rich milk and highly digestible meat, the massively powerful beak of a parrot, which exerts thousands of pounds of pressure for crushing food, the instinctual capacities of a dog, which help it find its way home from hundreds or perhaps thousands of miles away: how did it all develop? Who causes it all to work so effectively? If it is God, imagine this: to do all this and an infinite amount besides, how truly almighty He must be.

Consider the impact of such thinking. When a believer looks at the sky, he sees the workings of almighty God. When he beholds the star-filled heavens, he understands a portion of Him. When he sees a beautiful creature: a dove, a colored song bird, a loyal pet, a ferocious beast, a docile farm animal—in all he sees a part of God. If he studies their behavior and function, he understands Him even more profoundly. The more he looks, the more greatly he learns, and the more intensely he studies, the more in awe he becomes of God. Ultimately, he sees Him in every object and in every living being, even the lowly insect or microbe, even in a grain of sand.

In today's civilization the contributions of Islam are vast. These contributions may be recounted in the details, for instance, the Arabic numerals, the chemistry lab, the experimental method, modern mathematics, the laws of physics, the atlas, the encyclopedia, the almanac, social sophistication, the time piece, eyeglasses, fine tapestries, cotton clothing, the handkerchief, stained glass, colored ink, herbal medicine, essential oils, personal hygiene, and countless others. Yet, it was the way of thinking of Islam which produced the most profound results. This is because it created the very system that humans today hold so dear: a liberal, advanced civilization, one which places the needs of human beings as the top priority.

Usually, when civilizations falter, whatever they have produced involutes with them. Little if any of their achievements are transferred to the newcomers. Certainly, other civilizations may arise to some degree in the ruins of a previous one. Yet, the science and technology of the lost civilization are never directly transferred intact, not even remotely so. The ancient Greeks and Romans were excellent examples. No one directly inherited either their science or technology. Nor were the achievements of the Mayans or Incas adopted by others. All were lost. Thus, the new civilizations must invent their own ways. The same arduous processes of gradual advancement and discovery must be repeated. Islam changed this. For the first time in history existing civilizations inherited the learning of an advanced one, while the latter was still largely intact. Islam carefully delivered its magnificence to the Christian West. In contrast, today, now that Christianity, as well as Judaism, are massively powerful, they are applying their authority to disrupt the lands of Islam, destroying both its people and natural resources. This has resulted in the continued deaths of tens of millions of people. These lands are controlled, in fact, tyrannized, by Western puppets, who are installed, as well as maintained, with taxpayer's dollars. These rulers are imposed upon the people. Yet, who is the source of such impositions, such tyrannical regimes? It isn't Islam. Rather, it is the West. The fact is all of the rulers of down-trodden "Islamic Countries" are either Western or Eastern installed. This includes the rulers of Egypt, Libya, Morocco, Algeria, Syria, Iraq, Bahrain, Abu Dhabi, Kuwait, Qatar, and Turkey, as well as Saudi Arabia. What's more, regardless of which of the two are directly responsible, East or West, both work together to prevent Islam's rise. This is because they fear it. It is because Islam destroys all forms of corruption, vested interest, and selfish representations. Iran is the exception. This is because it is the only Middle Eastern country in which the people themselves vote for their ruler. Yet, every possible attempt is being made by both the West and East to destabilize, corrupt, and destroy this peoples' movement. The attempt is to represent Islam as a demonic force. It is an attempt which will ultimately fail.

Tyranny is never one sided. It negatively affects all civilization, including all monotheistic religions. Certainly, the powers-to-be of Christianity and Judaism fail to benefit by tyrannizing the lands of Islam. They can never benefit by alienating the people of other countries. This is because humanity is ultimately one brotherhood. All are dependent upon each other. All can benefit each other. If such a concept was truly practiced, there would be a dramatic change in this world. Human society would flourish in an unconceivably phenomenal way. Poverty-stricken countries would become productive. There would be a greater degree of happiness and security. People of all types could pursue their dreams and desires. What's more, there would be an improvement of global health, both for the planet and its inhabitants.

What a travesty it is that people of faith usually fail to find the common point. Christians, Jews, and Muslims should, theoretically, be the most peace-loving of all people. They should greatly get along. They should find their common ground. They should love each other as if brothers. This is far from an impossible feat. For instance, during the Islamic Era people of various faiths worked together to advance civilization. Yet, even today, the believers in God, whether Muslim, Christian, or Jew, have everything in common. All were given divine books. All were marked high by God. Ideally, all should work together to enhance the quality of life, for all people. All should strive as a singular group to make this world a superior, safer place. All should work in unison to prevent its destruction. Ultimately, genetically, they truly are brothers and sisters, arising from one father: Abraham. What's more, the original leaders of these faiths, Isaac, Ishmael, Solomon, David, Jesus (through the virgin Mary), and Muhammad, all arose from him. Thus, their leaders, that is their very prophets, are themselves blood brothers. Is there any other conclusion other than the fact that they should love and respect each other? David and Solomon are of the same lineage, the same genes and blood, of today's Jews, Christians, and Muslims. Then, isn't it sensible that such people find a brotherhood in faith? Shouldn't they naturally feel a compassion for each other—in fact, love—instead of mistrust, hostility, jealousy, and hate? What an incredible issue: that the people of the various divine books have the same heritage, that is the same genes, and, yet, they are destroying each other. It is a crime which will be eventually assessed: by God almighty Himself.

In Islam belief in God and scientific advancement are synonymous. Through this bond the seeker of knowledge can develop a broad view of both this world and the vast universe. Ultimately, this results in a security of thought. Thus, the doubts and confusion so common in the minds of today's scientists are eliminated. There develops a peace of mind through knowing Who is responsible for this vast universe and Who is the ultimate source of its powers. Furthermore, the seeker of truth can combine belief in God with the pursuit of science to better understand himself. The result will be a more secure, peaceful attitude toward life. What's more, he can apply this understanding to make this world a superior, healthier place.

Everyone will eventually die. There is no technology, no science, to escape it. This is why belief in God is so crucial. It provides precise answers for an unknown result, which science itself fails to explain. The fact is what will the individual do if he or she dies in disbelief and there truly is a God of resurrection? This would be a catastrophe beyond measure.

The sciences were created in an environment of God. Today, this approach can again be revived. The fact is it is crucial to do so. This is because belief in God instills a morality in science, which is sorely lacking. Because it lacks morality, whatever science produces, even if it is proven harmful, is aggressively instituted. For instance, a chemist synthesizes a new molecule. He determines its properties and uses. Next, he determines its marketability. Safety is rarely if ever the primary concern. Pesticides are a good example. The maker may regard such chemicals as potential money makers. Moral responsibility is never considered: corporate profits are the only issue. Thus, without proof of safety the chemical, a known poison, is sold. Eventually it is used globally. Years later, it is proven that it destroys life, killing entire species, perhaps ecosystems. The chemical produces cancer and other diseases, causing untold death and misery. It destroys rare plants and animals, disrupting entire ecosystems. It brings entire species to extinction. Ultimately, it contaminates the entire earth, causing irreparable harm. Despite these revelations no attempt is made to rectify the damage or remove the offending substance from the market. On the contrary, as long as it is profitable every effort is made to continue selling it. The issue of human, animal, or plant health is the least priority. The long-term ill effects are ignored. Only when it is determined that the toxicity is causing massive global damage is action taken against it. Yet, such a discovery is always belated. What's more, invariably, the fact is the potential for such damage is usually known in advance, yet, it is disregarded.

Belief in God creates a feeling of responsibility to Him. Such a belief is sorely lacking in the sciences. In the sciences this belief system once existed, specifically in the Islamic Empire of the 8th through 12th centuries. Then, scientific texts began with the words, "In the name of the most merciful God."

Scientific achievements have modernized the world. Yet, they are also destroying it. Advancements in the sciences can occur without destructive results. Only a moral science, that is a science based upon belief in an almighty and all-involved God, will reverse this crisis. Only a sense of responsibility, in fact, accountability, can create such changes. It is a crisis which must be reversed if there is any hope for the future generations as well as this planet itself.

Every effort should be made to reinstitute morality in science. The result will be a world in which the needs of the people and the planet are placed as the priority rather than the desires of the vested few. Islam produced the sciences, when in the Western world morality was at its lowest ebb. Now, it is time to reinstitute its principles. It would be an effort worthy of the finest of souls: to save the life of an entire planet and all who exist upon it.

Appendix

Qur'anic Translations

The Qur'an (pronounced Qur-aan, as if *Qur* and *aan* are separate words) was originally revealed in Arabic. The Arabic is utterly profound. However, initially, in studying it English translations are acceptable.

Currently, high-quality English translations are difficult to procure. The typical ones have numerous disadvantages, including a lack of accuracy. Many of these translations were accomplished by Western writers, who had no in-depth understanding of Islam. Others are seemingly archaic, written in old English and translated in the early part of this century or prior. Much could be done to improve such translations and, thus, there is an ongoing effort to do so. User friendly English translations are currently being developed.

The translations used by English-speaking Muslims are also cumbersome. The fact is many Muslims, perhaps the majority, only minimally understand the essence of this book.

Yet, the Qur'an was never meant to be a standard book. Certainly, it was never meant as a scholarly work. Rather, its purpose is to guide human beings. Therefore, to merely study it, like a scholarly text, defiles its purpose. In fact, there is little if any value in such an approach. Rather, it is meant to be internalized for the purpose of putting it into practice. The fact is it is meant to be put into action. It is that rare book which provides guidance whenever it is needed. Its only value is in abiding by its message. Its ultimate power is through internalizing its message in order to advance the self. In contrast, mere scholarly study and rote memorization are of little if any consequence. The Prophet himself warned against this. He said there would come a time when the Qur'an would be relegated to mere rhythmical chanting and decoration, while people failed to internalize it. This, he warned, would lead to the downfall of civilization. Thus, as proven by the Prophet all its power is derived from practicing it. Even practicing a tiny portion of it is superior to memorization. The fact is to become of the Qur'an in spirit and practice is the only obligation of the Muslim. Thus, the only true "Qur'anic scholars" are those who fully practice it in their daily lives. Therefore, the Qur'an is meant to be lived. It was created as a step-wise personal guide. Its purpose is to guide humankind. Its objective is to protect the human soul from its greatest deficiency: the lack of an understanding of which direction to follow in life. The Qur'an categorically solves this. It asks humans to follow God. It asks them to adhere to His rules.

Again, the Qur'an's purpose is to live it. It is to be studied only to be lived. The fact is its prophet warned against using it for pompous scholarship. Thus, to study it simply for the sake of becoming a "scholar" or "authority" defiles its purpose. Its prophet never claimed to be an imam, scholar, or sheik. The fact is such pompous scholarship neutralizes its powers, because it directly violates the Prophet's way. In other words, there is no sheik in Islam. True, leaders are critical. Yet, it is the example which matters. The best leader is the one who truly practices what he espouses. Thus, the spiritual leader in Islam is the one who is the most true in practice, not necessarily the most knowledgeable.

The Prophet never held himself as a religious authority. He accepted no pay for his role as spiritual leader. The fact is he was merely a human being like all others. The only difference was that he lived the Qur'an completely. Thus, the people supported him because of the kind of person he was. His superiority was that he practiced the Qur'an more thoroughly than anyone else. The fact is the Prophet Muhammad lived it to perfection. Thus, the Qur'an should be studied for personal development. Its message should be incorporated into daily living. What's more, the Prophet, may God rest his soul, should also be studied as a source of insight to understand it.

There is a method to studying the Qur'an. While it is directed at the individual and is meant for his or her own benefit, admittedly, in-depth scholarship and joint study may greatly aid in its understanding. Thus, it should ideally be studied with those who understand it and also practice it. The main issue is to find an individual who can explain the meaning of the Arabic terms. Ideally, the Arabic language should be learned. Yet, again, as it is studied it should be enacted. The way to do so is to become a living example of its message. This is the highest level the Qur'anic student can achieve.

Originally, the Qur'an was revealed in segments, some short, many of medium length, and others rather lengthy. The fact is it was meant to be understood immediately, that is as soon as it was revealed. What's more, it was meant to be utilized upon receipt. When it was first revealed, an effort was made by its recipients to master it. As it was revealed its followers memorized it. The purpose of this was so that its concepts could be incorporated immediately. The fact is the only way to truly understand it is to deeply consider its meaning, and then practice it. In order to appreciate its power it must be transformed into the person's daily living. In fact, it must become the entire structure of the individual. Anything less than this is regarded as a loss.

Its bearer, Prophet Muhammad, said little regarding it. Instead, he lived it. Like Christ, who was a living example of the Bible, Muhammad was a walking example of the Qur'an. The fact is when people asked him to teach them the Qur'an, he told them, essentially, "Study me: I represent it." Thus, obviously, from its bearer's point of view it is meant strictly for personal improvement.

Some people use the Qur'an as a means to evaluate right and wrong. They may even use it to judge others. This is never its purpose. It is meant to support the human race, never to instigate pain or harm. True, it contains principles of behavior, even prohibitions. Yet, these rules are utterly basic, for instance, "don't kill a person wrongfully, that is unless in defense of being tyrannized, don't commit adultery, don't harm your fellow man, don't tyrannize, cheat, steal, and/or incite corruption." These are rules which every civilized human being realizes and which each person is under an obligation to follow. Instinctively, it seems, human beings realize such acts are wrong. Yet, while the Qur'an is a clear reminder, it is never meant as a tool for judging or incriminating others. Rather, it is meant as a personal tool: for advancing the self and for gaining the maximum advantages, especially for the life to come. It is to be used for the aforementioned purpose. It should never be used to incriminate or judge others. Rather, it is a guide to improve or elevate the self.

Today, people who desire its message are faced with a dilemma. This is the fact that the Qur'an is a massive book. In contrast, when it was first recorded it was studied in segments until the meaning was thoroughly understood. Many people find it difficult to read a mere article or novel let alone a huge book. Yet, there is no need to be overwhelmed. The Qur'an is meant only as guidance. Thus, it is unnecessary to read it cover to cover. However, initially, it is helpful to read it thoroughly, starting from the beginning. Even so, for use on demand it is sufficient to open it randomly. In fact, it is possible to pray over it and simply open it. There are pearls throughout, and experience has demonstrated God will guide the individual directly regarding what he or she needs. The person may page through it until the search proves fruitful. Usually, as a result, guidance will be found.

The Qur'an can be studied systematically. Plus, help can be found. For those seeking its proper interpretation it is important not to talk to just anyone. Not every person of "Muslim" heritage understands it or even practices it. The only ones who can truly help are those who themselves truly and fully practice it. They are those who are essentially living Qur'ans and who truly represent its meaning in their own lives.

Think about the consequences of seeking such advice. Regarding a critical issue a person ideally would only ask for aid from an expert. Any lesser approach could result in disaster. Could there be any issue more crucial than the meeting with almighty God? The point is for such a critical issue, attempt to find the most sincere, brilliant expert available. Find someone who truly understands and follows the Qur'an. Only such a person could give proper advice.

There is another dilemma: poor translations. The fact is a poor translation may prove cumbersome. It could frustrate even the most sincere attempts at achieving an understanding. In other words, such an insufficient or, perhaps, misconstrued document may utterly fail to transmit the true essence of this book, as found in the Arabic original. In fact, certain of the translations are so inadequate that little if any serious guidance can be procured. Even so, there is a translation which may prove useful. It is M. Asad's *The Message of the Qur'an*. This is a large and expensive volume. Mr. Asad was a European who in the 1920s discovered Islam. He became fluent in Arabic and, therefore, translated the Qur'an. While it uses many old fashioned and old English words, it is accurate and inspiring. This is because Mr. Asad had a thorough understanding of Arabic. Plus, as is evident from his translation and commentary his effort was monumental as well as sincere. Truly, he put his full heart and soul into it. When reading this translation, there is a sense of an effort devoted exclusively to the service of God. In other words, every effort was made to represent the true meaning. This is why, currently, this translation is superior to all others. However, it is largely a scholarly work and, therefore, often requires explanation. Plus, it is written in a style of English which is cumbersome.

The Qur'an cannot be treated flippantly. It is a serious book. Translations which contain Arabic require special consideration. This is because the Arabic is pure, unaltered divine text. It is a type of holy writing. The Arabic script should never be taken into a toilet. To read the Arabic requires a shower or the Islamic wash known as *wudu*. However, this is unnecessary when reading the translation. When reading, touching or reciting the Arabic, proper hygiene is required. The hands should be washed and the genitals free of urine or feces. Currently, the Asad translation contains Arabic.

This translation is unavailable in traditional bookstores. It may be ordered at specialty bookstores. If it is unavailable, contact Knowledge House at 1-800-295-3737. The cost is $45.00 plus $9.95 shipping and handling.

This translation has a thorough commentary, which may prove valuable for the novice.

Additionally, an exclusively English translation has recently been developed. This American edition is easy to read and understand. This is the ideal translation for beginners. There is no Arabic in this text, making it convenient for English readers. Entitled *the Magnificent Message* for Americans this is the preferred translation. In contrast to the Asad translation it requires little or no explanation. Thus, the individual may largely study it independently. Plus, it is free of Arabic. To purchase it contact:

The Magnificent Message
c/o Knowledge House Publishers
P. O. Box 855
Buffalo Grove, IL 60089
1-800-295-3737

The Qur'an is an invaluable document. With a good translation and knowledgeable help it is relatively easy to understand.

Ideally, a knowledge of Arabic aids in its study. This is because the Qur'an was revealed in Arabic. However, the essence of its meaning may be readily translated. Thus, even in other languages with careful study the message can be determined. However, to properly do so, qualified help is often required. Yet, the new American edition is largely self-explanatory.

To thoroughly gain its benefits an effort is required. Simply glossing over it fails to elucidate its true meaning.

The individual must read it with full attention, that is with the heart attuned to its meaning. This effort may require a combination of a well written English translation (i.e. Asad's translation or the *Magnificent Message*) along with supportive help from a true believer. Many mosques have available sincere individuals, who can assist in properly understanding the text. Yet, regarding the latter relatively few individuals possess an in-depth understanding of its message.

There is another reason the Qur'an is unique. This is because it fails to relate to only one time period. Rather, it adapts with the phases of human history, molding itself to the most current needs and thinking. In this respect, truly, the Qur'an is a miracle. This further indicates the need for a modern, that is current, translation. The Arabic words are highly versatile. A single word could have dozens, even hundreds, of meanings.

The Qur'an possesses an essence that is devoid in other books. It is an essence which demands a celestial source. It is also an essence which implies a lack of human corruption. Even to the novice or, perhaps, antagonist it truly appears to have a non-human origin. The fact that it offers the ability to guide human beings clearly indicates the probability of an extraterrestrial origin. In its own words its objective is the guidance of humankind.

The Qur'an contains a wide range of practical information, which is useful both for personal and social growth. It contains rules, which are of value in the creation of a liberal, refined, and law-abiding civilization. It establishes relatively few prohibitions. These prohibitions are similar to the Ten Commandments. However, its ultimate value is in its message, which is directed to humans individually. It is a message for reviving and guiding human souls. It is also a message for preparing them both for proper behavior in this life and the successful transition into the final life. The Qur'an teaches the individual how to serve the almighty Lord. Its premise is simple. Without God, that is without His in-depth guidance, humankind will self-destruct. He wishes to prevent this in every conceivable way, so He instructs his servants how to avoid this. What's more, this self destruction will occur sooner than anyone could possibly imagine, perhaps within this lifetime. The only solution—the only hope—is for humankind to turn to God en masse. It is to love and worship Him, strictly for His sake. It is to abandon every self-centered, conceited attitude for the responsibility of serving the almighty Lord. It is to halt the unbridled destruction of this planet. It is to worship Him lovingly. It is to abide by His every desire. It is to do good deeds for His sake. It is also to avoid blatantly damaging this planet and its creatures. This is the way of life edified in the Qur'an. It is the true definition of Islam.

The Qur'an indicates that the earth, or at least the livable portion of it, will ultimately be destroyed. The indication is that it will be through an astronomical event. In numerous sections it describes a crushing global disaster. This will happen while it is fully inhabited. Perhaps through a firm dedication to His way and an unbridled effort to combat evil this imminent doom could be delayed. Perhaps it could be thwarted. Yet, what is certain is that evil has gained the advantage over good. The purpose of Islam is to reverse this trend. Its purpose is to defeat all forms of evil. Yet, evil is defined as any force which harms the creatures of this planet as well as the planet itself.

Because Islam is a force for good, it must be investigated. The world is in need of good. The fact is evil has overwhelmed it. Throughout history Islam has promoted in fact, created, the good, that is the productive and useful. It was directly responsible for the majority of this world's modern advances: algebra, arithmetic, trigonometry, astronomy, chemistry, biology, medicine, pharmacology, herbal medicine, aromatherapy, geography, geology, physics, and much more. Thus, its principles should be cultivated, never obstructed. Through it this world can be saved. It is a challenge worthy of pursuing. By doing so, the rewards will be immense, both in this life and the next. Certainly, the individual will be enormously rewarded. He will feel peace at heart, a peace so elusive in today's world, because he is certain he is on the right path. This is because he has found the way to serve God at the highest level. It is because he has a certainty: that peace and confidence of knowing the divine truths. It is because he will seek to serve God, even before his own self. It is because he will strive to make God's rules the authority on this earth rather than the rules of mortal men. This challenge to establish the rule of God is worthy of any effort. By joining His team and by accepting

His rule the individual chooses a most profound goal: the struggle of good against evil and the battle of morality against tyranny. It is a most worthy cause, one of great and profound heights, which will create a sense of purpose as well as positive results. It is the purpose of serving the greater good. It is the objective to improve the quality of life for all living creatures, as well as the planet itself, which is precisely what Islam stands for.

Bibliography

Asad, M. *The Message of the Qur'an*. Gibraltar: Dar al-Andalus.

Briffault, Robert. 1930. *Rational Evolution*. New York: Macmillion.

Goldstein, T. 1980. *Dawn of Modern Science*. Boston: Houghton Mifflin Co.

Hitti, P. 1943. *The Arabs: a Short History*. Princeton: Princeton Univ. Press.

Husaini, S. W. Ahmed. 1995. *Astronomical Sciences in the Qur'an*. Delhi: Karakush Publishers.

Jastrow, Robert. 2000. *God and the Astronomers*. Norton, W. W. & Company, Inc.

Kennedy, D. (ed). 1962. *The Living Cell*. San Francisco: W. H. Freeman and Co.

Khaleel, Kasem. 2003. *The True Origins of Modern Science*. Buffalo Grove: Knowledge House.

Khaleel, Kasem. 2002. *The Magnificent Message: Guidance for Humankind* (preliminary manuscript). Buffalo Grove: Knowledge House.

Maududi, S. A. 1970. *Towards Understanding Islam*. Karachi.

Pasha, S. H., Ph.D. Personal communication.

Rashed, R. (ed). *Encyclopedia of the History of Arabic Science*. V. 2. London: Routledge

Smith, B. 1996. *Spain: A History in Art*. Madrid. Gemini, Inc.

Smoot, G. and K. Davidson. 1993. *Wrinkles in Time*. New York: William Morrow and Co.

Taylor, Gordon R. 1983. *Great Evolution Mystery*. Harper Collins

Taylor, Walt. 1933. *Arabic Words in English*. Oxford.

Turner, H. 1997. *Science in Medieval Islam*. Austin: University of Texas Press.

Index

Books

#1 *Science in the Name of God*
— $19.95 each U.S. $29.95 Canada
336 pages   5.5 x 8.5 inch softbound   ISBN 1-931078-05-X
Have we been taught true history? Is Newton and Galileo's fame based upon fables? Which cultures were the true sources of modern science — Eastern or Western? How could the West produce it if it was immersed in the dark ages? Was Di Vinci merely a painter and designer, never a scientist? Learn the real origins of modern science as well as discoveries like the telescope, compass, time pieces, eye glasses, modern mathematics, modern medicine, and more. Finally, learn the truth after centuries of mis information.

#2 *The Incredible Qur'an*— $10.95 each U.S. $12.95 Canada
169 pages   5.5 x 8.5 inch softbound   ISBN 0-911119-54-X
Multiple-choice and other questions useful for teaching both adults and students. Great for grade and high schoolers.

ORDER FORM

Item		Quantity	Amount

Books

Book #1 ***Science in the Name of God*** —
              $19.95 each*   _____   _____

Book #2 ***Science and Religion*** — $14.95 each*   _____   _____

Book #3 ***The Incredible Qur'an*** — $10.95 each*   _____   _____

            Sub-Total   _____

            Sales Tax (if any)   _____

            Shipping*   _____

            TOTAL   _____

*Shipping Charges: $6.00 for single books—add $2.00 for each additional boo
Payment by check, money order, or credit card.

Make checks payable to: Knowledge House
                              P.O. Box 4885
                              Buffalo Grove, IL 60089

                              Telephone: (800) 243-5242

Use the following for VISA, Mastercard or American Express orders:

Credit Card # _____ Exp. Date _____

Name _____

Address _____

City _____State _____Zip_____

NOTES

NOTES

NOTES